Standardized Testing

by Carla Mooney

LUCENT BOOKS

A part of Gale, Cengage Learning

GALE
CENGAGE Learning

Farmington Hills, Mich • San Francisco • New York • Waterville, Maine
Meriden, Conn • Mason, Ohio • Chicago

LIBRARY OF CONGRESS CATALOGING-IN-PUBLICATION DATA

Mooney, Carla, 1970-
  Standardized testing / by Carla Mooney.
    pages cm. -- (Hot topics)
  Includes bibliographical references and index.
  ISBN 978-1-4205-1241-0 (hardcover)
  1. Educational tests and measurements--United States--Juvenile literature.
  I. Title.
  LB3051.M778 2015
  371.26--dc23

                                                          2015004493

Lucent Books
27500 Drake Rd.
Farmington Hills, MI 48331

ISBN-13: 978-1-4205-1241-0
ISBN-10: 1-4205-1241-2

Printed in the United States of America
1 2 3 4 5 6 7 19 18 17 16 15

CONTENTS

FOREWORD

Young people today are bombarded with information. Aside from traditional sources such as newspapers, television, and the radio, they are inundated with a nearly continuous stream of data from electronic media. They send and receive e-mails and instant messages, read and write online "blogs," participate in chat rooms and forums, and surf the web for hours. This trend is likely to continue. As Patricia Senn Breivik, the former dean of university libraries at Wayne State University in Detroit, has stated, "Information overload will only increase in the future. By 2020, for example, the available body of information is expected to double every 73 days! How will these students find the information they need in this coming tidal wave of information?"

Ironically, this overabundance of information can actually impede efforts to understand complex issues. Whether the topic is abortion, the death penalty, gay rights, or obesity, the deluge of fact and opinion that floods the print and electronic media is overwhelming. The news media report the results of polls and studies that contradict one another. Cable news shows, talk radio programs, and newspaper editorials promote narrow viewpoints and omit facts that challenge their own political biases. The World Wide Web is an electronic minefield where legitimate scholars compete with the postings of ordinary citizens who may or may not be well-informed or capable of reasoned argument. At times, strongly worded testimonials and opinion pieces both in print and electronic media are presented as factual accounts.

Conflicting quotes and statistics can confuse even the most diligent researchers. A good example of this is the question of whether or not the death penalty deters crime. For instance, one study found that murders decreased by nearly one-third when the death penalty was reinstated in New York in 1995. Death penalty supporters cite this finding to support their argument that the existence of the death penalty deters criminals from committing murder. However, another study found that states without the death penalty have murder rates below the national average. This study is cited by opponents of capital punishment, who reject the claim that the death penalty deters murder. Students need context and clear, informed discussion if they are to think critically and make informed decisions.

The Hot Topics series is designed to help young people wade through the glut of fact, opinion, and rhetoric so that they can think critically about controversial issues. Only by reading and thinking critically will they be able to formulate a viewpoint that is not simply the parroted views of others. Each volume of the series focuses on one of today's most pressing social issues and provides a balanced overview of the topic. Carefully crafted narrative, fully documented primary and secondary source quotes, informative sidebars, and study questions all provide excellent starting points for research and discussion. Full-color photographs and charts enhance all volumes in the series. With its many useful features, the Hot Topics series is a valuable resource for young people struggling to understand the pressing issues of the modern era.

INTRODUCTION

STANDARDIZED TESTING

In January 2013 teachers at Garfield High School in Seattle, Washington, voted unanimously to boycott the Measures of Academic Progress (MAP) standardized test. Adopted in the 2009–2010 school year, the MAP test measures reading and math skills and is designed to track student, teacher, and school progress. Along with hundreds of school systems in Washington State and other states, Seattle schools have administered the MAP test three times a year since 2009. Garfield teachers protested the MAP test because they said it was not aligned with the state's curriculum. As a result, they argued the test produced meaningless results that were being used to evaluate students, teachers, and schools. In a letter explaining the reasons for the boycott, the Garfield teachers wrote:

> We are professionals who care deeply about our students and cannot continue to participate in a practice that harms our school and our students. We want to be able to identify student growth and determine if our practice supports student learning. We wish to be evaluated in a way so that we can continue to improve our practice, and we wish for our colleagues who are struggling to be identified and either be supported or removed. The MAP test is not the way to do any of these things. We feel strongly that we must decline to give the MAP test even one more time.[1]

One of the primary problems the teachers cited with the test was that it did not assess students based on the curriculum taught in a specific grade level. "In 26 years of teaching," says

Kit McCormick, a Garfield English teacher, "this is the first time I've said, 'I'm not giving this test.' It's not that I think my ninth-graders should not be tested. I want my ninth-graders to be tested. I teach to the Common Core standards, and I am happy to teach those standards. Bottom line is: The test is not useful to my students."[2] The Northwest Evaluation Association, creator of the MAP test, defended the test, saying it quickly gives schools a reliable and fair progress report of student's individual aptitudes and progress.

Within several weeks of the Garfield boycott, teachers at six other Seattle schools joined the MAP boycott. Many parents and students also supported the teachers, staging rallies and opting out of the winter tests. As the boycott gained state and national attention, the Garfield teachers received support from the nationwide education community. Numerous teachers sent messages of encouragement. One Florida teacher sent several hot pizzas at lunchtime one day as a gesture of support. "It was a powerful moment," says history teacher Jesse Hagopian, one of the boycott's leaders. "That's when we realized this wasn't just a fight at Garfield; this was something going on across the nation. If we back down, we're not just backing away from a fight for us. It's something that educators all over see as their struggle too. I think a lot of teachers steeled their resolve, that we had to continue."[3]

In response to the teacher boycott, José Banda, Seattle Public Schools superintendent, created a task force of teachers, principals, parents, and community leaders to investigate the test and how it was being used in the district. In May 2013 Banda announced that according to the task force's recommendations, Seattle high schools would not have to administer the MAP test. The district would still administer the test at its elementary and middle schools. "There was opportunity here, and we hope to continue to have these conversations," says Banda. "We're listening to them and we're doing our best to support them in carrying out the work that needs to happen."[4]

After the announcement, the teachers celebrated. "When we got word that the superintendent had relented and acknowledged that this test was wrong for our students, there was a moment of pure elation," says Hagopian. "There were high fives and fist pumps in the hallway between teachers and students."[5] Other teachers, such as reading teacher Mallory Clarke, were more reserved about the announcement. Says Clarke:

> It's recognition of our professional power, but I fear it was not an acknowledgement of the rightness of our arguments. They have yet to answer any of our criticisms of the test. They told us it was invalid, but they are still willing to use the MAP at the elementary and middle school level. The Department of Education says the MAP has no value. Still, they are willing to spend money on it when we are hurting so badly for funds.[6]

The controversy in Seattle over the MAP test is one example of the growing national debate over standardized tests in schools. In the past few decades, standardized tests have become

The primary problem with standardized testing, according to teachers, is that it does not assess students on the basis of curriculum taught at a specific grade level.

part of every student's, teacher's, and school's life. While many believe that standardized tests are an important part of ensuring a fair and quality education to all students, others believe that standardized tests have become too large a part in assessing school, student, and teacher performance. As the debate intensifies, many expect more protests to emerge in schools and communities across the country. Says Hagopian, "We are just seeing the very beginning of this testing revolt."[7]

CHAPTER 1

HISTORY OF STANDARDIZED TESTING

Over the past century, standardized testing has been increasingly used in the America's public schools to assess student aptitudes and achievement. Standardized tests are defined as any test that is administered, scored, and interpreted in a standard, predetermined way. They are usually given to large groups of students across a state or country. They are different than regular spelling or science tests that are created by an individual teacher. Instead, standardized tests require all test takers to answer the same questions or a selection of questions from a common question bank. The tests are often scored by a computer, which allows them to be graded quickly and without bias. Because all students receive the same questions and scoring, the test scores can be easily compared among students.

The format of standardized tests is typically very similar. To make standardized tests easier to administer and grade, they often use a multiple-choice format. Some tests also include true-false questions and short-answer questions. Traditionally, students have used pencils to complete paper tests, although many schools are beginning to use computers to administer tests.

Standardized tests scores are used in many ways. Some tests determine if a child is ready for kindergarten. Other tests identify students who need special-education services or academic support. Standardized tests are used to place students in different course levels. States use standardized test scores to compare districts and schools. Many schools use student test scores to evaluate teachers' job performance. Colleges rely on test scores as a tool to evaluate prospective students.

Early History

Standardized tests have a long history in the American education system and around the world. The earliest known standardized tests were taken by government job applicants in seventh-century Imperial China. In use until the late 1800s, these tests evaluated an applicant's knowledge of Confucian philosophy. In the West standardized tests in schools appeared during the Industrial Revolution. The use of efficient machines to work in fields and factories allowed young farmhands and factory workers to return to school. Schools used standardized tests to assess their growing student population efficiently and quickly.

In the United States school reformers Horace Mann and Samuel Gridley Howe introduced standardized testing in Boston

School reformer Horace Mann introduced standardized testing in Boston public schools in the mid-1800s.

public schools in the mid-1800s. The men designed the new tests to provide a standard to judge and compare the performance of each school and to gather objective information about the quality of teachers. Boston's system of standardized testing quickly spread to school systems across the nation. Not everyone, however, was happy with the testing. In 1906 a New York State Education Department official commented to the state legislature:

> It is a great and more serious evil, by too frequent and too numerous examinations, so to magnify their importance that students come to regard them not as a means in education but as the final purpose, the ultimate goal. It is a very great and more serious evil to sacrifice systematic instruction and a comprehensive view of the subject for the scrappy and unrelated knowledge gained by students who are persistently drilled in the mere answering of questions issued by the Education department or other governing bodies.[8]

In Kansas the standardized test further evolved with the introduction of the first known published multiple-choice test in 1914. The Kansas Silent Reading Test was developed by Frederick J. Kelly, a Kansas school director. Kelly created the multiple-choice test to reduce the time and effort it took schools to administer and score tests.

Modern Testing Era

In the 1950s and 1960s, a national space race between the United States and the Soviet Union increased pressure on American schools to show improvement and achievement. In 1965 President Lyndon Johnson signed the Elementary and Secondary Education Act (ESEA). The ESEA included standardized testing provisions in an effort to make schools more accountable for quality and the needs of all students. The tests were used to make sure all students graduated with at least the ability to read and do basic math. If students did not pass the tests required under the ESEA, they might not receive a diploma. Teachers and schools faced no consequences tied to student test scores. Eventually, criticism mounted that the ESEA tests were too easy to pass and were not challenging students enough.

In the years after the ESEA, concern over the American public school system grew. Some people believed that international schools were superior to American schools. In 1983 the National Commission on Excellence in Education released a report, *A Nation at Risk: The Imperative for Educational Reform*, which warned that American schools urgently needed to raise academic standards or risk America's future economic security. The report found that student test scores were rapidly declining, while low teacher salaries and poor teacher training programs led to a high turnover rate. At the same time, other countries threatened to surpass America's technological superiority. The report cited statistical evidence—23 million American adults were functionally illiterate, and only one-fifth of seventeen-year-old students were able to write a persuasive essay. The report also found that outdated classroom learning allowed students to advance through school with minimal effort. "When the report came out, it catapulted the issue of education onto the national agenda," says Mary Hatwood Futrell, professor and dean of the George Washington University Graduate School of Education and Human Development in Washington, D.C., and former president of the National Education Association. "I can remember when it came out and it didn't matter if you were looking at the morning news, the afternoon news, magazines, newspapers, it was everywhere. And no one anticipated that it was going to have that kind of impact."[9]

CHANGING EDUCATION

"What are we testing, and how are we doing it? What I think is that we're doing way too much of this testing, and it is changing the way in which we educate our children."—Ron Berler, a journalist who spent a year observing how students and educators handled standardized testing

Quoted in Brooke Berger. "Don't Teach to the Test." *U.S. News & World Report*, April 11, 2013. www.usnews.com/opinion/articles/2013/04/11/why-excessive-standardized-testing-is-causing-american-schools-to-fail.

Automated Test Scoring

In 1931 high school physics teacher and inventor Reynold B. Johnson from Ironwood, Michigan, began to experiment with designing an electrical machine to grade his students' tests. Before automated machines, test scoring was entirely manual. A scorer read each pencil mark on the test paper and calculated a score. To automate scoring, Johnson designed a machine that could detect pencil marks on an answer sheet using tiny electrical circuits. The machine then compared the marks to an answer key.

In 1934 a company called International Business Machines (IBM) hired Johnson to create a production model of his test scoring machine. Three years later IBM launched Johnson's machine as the world's first automatic test scoring machine, the IBM 805. The IBM 805 graded answer sheets using electrical current flowing through graphite pencil marks. The new machine greatly increased the speed and efficiency of test scoring. An experienced operator inserted answer sheets into the machine and recorded the resulting scores. An experienced operator using the IBM 805 could score about eight hundred to one thousand sheets per hour.

Although the IBM 805 was no longer marketed after 1963, automated scoring technology continues today. Instead of using electrical current through graphite pencil marks, today's modern scanners use optical mark technology that recognizes marks from pens and pencils when scoring standardized tests.

An IBM employee demonstrates the IBM test scoring machine.

The report received a mountain of media attention and renewed interest in how American public schools educated their students. Education reform advocates called for stricter school and teacher accountability measures, which included increased standardized testing. In 2002 President George W. Bush signed the No Child Left Behind Act (NCLB) into law. For the first time, public schools were required to track and measure student achievement. The law required states to develop and implement challenging academic standards for reading and math and set state progress goals to ensure all students achieved proficiency in these subjects by 2014. To measure achievement, NCLB mandated that states test all public school students annually in grades 3 through 8. For the first time, schools faced consequences if students did not perform well on the tests. If a school did not show Adequate Yearly Progress toward the state objectives, it faced sanctions or corrective action. As a result of NCLB, standardized testing and test-based accountability have become the norm in American schools. The act also focused attention on low-performing students and schools, forcing educators to come up with plans to improve performance.

In 2009 President Barack Obama signed another educational reform, the Race to the Top program, into law. The program invited states to compete for $4.35 billion in additional funding by making reforms that improve teaching and learning in American schools, as measured by their student test scores. "The $4.35 billion Race to the Top program that we are unveiling today is a challenge to states and districts. We're looking to drive reform, reward excellence and dramatically improve our nation's schools,"[10] said Secretary of Education Arne Duncan at a press conference to announce the program. The U.S. Department of Education credits the Race to the Top program with prompting more than one hundred state laws since 2009 that require schools to raise educational standards and revise teacher evaluation systems.

Types of Standardized Testing

Today many types of standardized tests are used in schools across the United States. Some of the most common standardized tests are achievement tests, aptitude tests, and college admissions tests. Achievement tests are used to measure the knowledge and skills students have learned in school. For example, Advanced Placement (AP) tests are used to measure how well a student has learned material presented during an AP course. In Pennsylvania the Keystone Exams are end-of-course assessment tests in certain content areas such as algebra I, biology, and literature. Other state achievement tests are used to measure the academic progress students have made year after year. In Pennsylvania students in grades 3 through 8 take the Pennsylvania System of School Assessment (PSSA) tests in language arts and mathematics annually. Students in grades 4 and 8 also take science PSSA tests. Like Pennsylvania, many states and school districts administer their version of achievement tests annually. Some schools may use achievement tests to determine if a student is ready for an advanced course or if he or she needs additional academic support. Achievement test results are also being used to evaluate the effectiveness of schools and teachers.

Instead of evaluating what a student has already learned, aptitude tests attempt to predict a student's ability in a particular skill, such as math skills, language proficiency, abstract reasoning, or musical talent. Aptitude tests are used to predict how a student will do in a future school or class setting. Schools administer aptitude tests to determine a student's placement in a particular course or if he or she qualifies for more intensive reading support. Aptitude tests can also predict success in future careers and courses of study. Many middle and high school students take the Differential Aptitude Test, a career aptitude test that tests students on verbal reasoning, numerical ability, abstract reasoning, mechanical reasoning, and spatial relations. The test assesses students' ability to acquire future skills and suggests career and educational options based on students' strengths and weaknesses.

Generations of high school students have prepared for college by taking the SAT exam administered by the College Board or the ACT administered by ACT, Inc. These two tests have become very important factors for college admissions decisions, particularly for the most competitive colleges. Many college admissions officers use ACT and SAT test scores as indicators of

Algebra I End-of-Course Exam

This report provides information about your student's performance on the American Diploma Project (ADP) Algebra I End-of-two purposes: to determine whether a student has mastered algebra content and whether the student is prepared for higher-this exam, including the subscores, will help students identify areas of weakness so that they can improve their skills and pre students complete Algebra I, they should continue to take courses for which Algebra I is a prerequisite. The most important th mathematics is to take mathematics courses during all four years of high school.

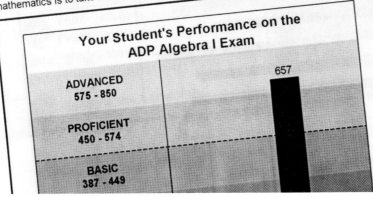

Your Student's Performance on the ADP Algebra I Exam

657

ADVANCED
575 - 850

PROFICIENT
450 - 574

BASIC
387 - 449

Performance Levels

Advanced - The student cor and skills needed to show m effective at devising and clea strategies to solve complex The student computes accu symbolic language to solve The student's explanations reasoning to justify solution

Proficient - The student u skills to show adequate p The student is usually eff

The most common standardized tests are achievement tests, aptitude tests, and college admissions tests.

academic potential and how well applicants will do in college programs. In recent years, however, a debate over the accuracy and usefulness of these tests has increased, and several colleges have eliminated the tests from their application requirements. Beyond college, graduate schools often require applicants to take specialized standardized tests such as the Graduate Record Examination (GRE) or the graduate tests for law (LSAT), business (GMAT), or medicine (MCAT).

Test Results

For many years test scores have been used to evaluate individual students. Test scores indicate whether students have learned what they are expected to learn and whether they meet state learning standards. Test scores can also reveal gaps in student learning and academic progress. Teachers and schools can use this information to create an individual learning plan for the student. Schools also use standardized test scores to determine additional needs such as whether a student should be admitted to a gifted program or whether he or she needs to receive remedial instruction. For colleges test scores on college entrance exams are part of a student's application, which determines whether or not a student is accepted.

In recent years test scores have done more than evaluate individual students. Administrators and state officials have put an increased emphasis on using standardized tests to evaluate teachers, schools, and entire districts. By comparing test scores among teachers, schools, and districts, administrators and other officials can compare the performance of each. Standardized tests are also being used to identify achievement gaps between different groups of students, such as students of different races, ethnic backgrounds, and economic backgrounds. When achievement gaps are identified for a particular group of students, educators can make changes to policies and programs to address the needs

Many high school students are tested for college admissions by taking the SAT exam, a standardized test.

of this student group. Elected officials also look to standardized tests to evaluate whether legislation, public programs, and other policies are working as intended. They can use results to support efforts to introduce new legislation or programs designed to improve the American public education system.

Growth of High-Stakes Testing

As the ways standardized tests are used has expanded, the stakes have increased for many involved in the public school system. These high-stakes tests are being used to make increasingly important decisions about students, teachers, schools, and districts, which carry significant consequences. High scores are often rewarded. A high-scoring student may be passed to the next grade level or placed in an advanced class. Teachers with high-scoring classes receive better evaluations, which can lead to higher raises and future promotions. High-scoring schools and districts receive positive publicity when scores are published in local newsletters and can qualify for additional funding from the state and federal government.

On the other hand, low scores on high-stakes tests can have negative consequences. Students who receive low scores may be held back or denied a diploma. Teachers of low-scoring classes may see their evaluation scores suffer, receive lower pay raises, or even be fired. Low-scoring schools and districts can face state sanctions, interventions, and possible closure.

The increase in high-stakes testing is also costing schools financially. After the passage of NCLB, initial tests revealed significant achievement gaps between white and minority students in many schools. In response many states developed interventions to help struggling students and also expanded standardized testing programs. Through the 1990s and 2000s, states added more tests, including standardized assessment in algebra, chemistry, history, and in some cases physical fitness. The new tests came with a significant cost. In Florida the average amount spent on testing per student was about five dollars in 1997. The cost per student surged to twenty-two dollars in 2012. In Pennsylvania the cost of testing students multiplied by five times between 2003 and 2012, even as the enrollment in public schools declined. In Texas assessment costs are projected to reach $99 million for the 2014–2015 school year.

Multibillion-Dollar Industry

Today standardized testing has become a multibillion-dollar industry in the United States. According to a 2012 report released by the Brown Center on Education Policy at the Brookings Institution, researchers estimate that standardized testing regimens cost states about $1.7 billion annually. Based on data from forty-four states and the District of Columbia, the report calculated that states spend an average of sixty-five dollars per student in grades 3 to 9 for testing. Matthew Chingos, Brown Center fellow and the report's author, says that testing costs will become more difficult for schools to pay for as states face budget shortfalls and difficulties.

GOOD TESTS IMPROVE OUTCOMES

"Tests are not inherently damaging to instruction. In fact, a good test will improve student outcomes by helping teachers target instruction. And effective tests are surely necessary to gauge student progress."—Celine Coggins, founder and chief executive officer of Teach Plus, a nonprofit organization dedicated to improving educational outcomes for urban children

Celine Coggins. "Debate over Standardized Testing Is Focusing on the Wrong Questions." *Christian Science Monitor*, April 3, 2014. www.csmonitor.com/Commentary /Opinion/2014/0403/Debate-over-standardized-testing-is-focusing-on-the-wrong -questions.

Pearson, one of the world's largest for-profit education companies, administers more than 40 million tests annually. In 2011 Pearson scored more than 124 million tests, including tests created by other companies. The company works with eighteen states, Washington, D.C., and Puerto Rico. In Texas alone Pearson has a five-year testing contract, which generates revenue of nearly $500 million. "We consider it a privilege to serve students across K–12 and higher education,"[11] says Pearson spokesperson Jason Gaber. Other large testing companies include CTB/ McGraw-Hill and Riverside Publishing.

Critics of the standardized testing industry say that testing companies are primarily concerned with company profits instead of student achievement. "Test companies are profiting off the political mania of more testing,"[12] says Monty Neill, executive director of the National Center for Fair & Open Testing, also known as FairTest, an organization that promotes the fair evaluations of students, teachers, and schools. Others, such as Linda Kolbert, cofounder of Fund Education Now, a nonprofit advocacy group in Florida, agree and say that testing companies have lobbied politicians for more testing with profits in mind. "We can look at what [testing companies] are paying in lobbying fees," says Kolbert. "And I am sure you will see this as a big driver in the trend toward more testing."[13]

Testing Assessment Dollars Compared with Total Education Spending

Average dollars spent per student in seven representative states.

State	Total Per-Pupil Expenditure	Cost of Testing
California	$14	$8,955
Florida	$21	$8,578
Illinois	$13	$11,197
Massachusetts	$28	$13,055
Ohio	$38	$10,500
Rhode Island	$15	$15,024
Washington	$47	$9,928

Taken from: Education Sector at American Institutes for Research.

Do Tests Measure What Matters?

Does improving scores on standardized tests really matter? According to a 2013 study by researchers at the Massachusetts Institute of Technology (MIT), Harvard University, and Brown University, improving standardized test scores may not make a difference in a student's cognitive ability. In the study, researchers followed nearly fourteen hundred eighth-grade students in Boston public schools. They found that even when schools raised students' test scores on state standardized tests, the students did not experience a re-lated increase in fluid intelligence, which requires logical thinking and problem solving. Instead, researchers found that improving test scores raised the students' crystallized intelligence, or their ability to recalling previously learned facts from long-term memory. John Gabrielli, a professor of brain and cognitive sciences at MIT and the study's senior author, says that learning facts is important but that educators should use information from the study to adapt testing practices to help students improve cognitive abilities.

Growing Debate

Many test experts and educators believe that modern standardized testing is a fair and objective way to assess students' academic achievement. They assert the tests' standardized format and computerized scoring removes favoritism, bias, and subjectivity from student evaluations. In addition, supporters point out that regular standardized testing holds teachers and schools accountable to the public. They assert that states and taxpayers who are spending billions of dollars annually for public schools have a right to know if teachers and schools are meeting defined standards. "Parents are measuring and testing their children all their lives, from when they're born and we start weighing them to see if their growth is on target," says Doug Kubach, the chief executive officer of Pearson's testing division. "Assessments play the same role in the education world."[14] Because all students across a state take the same test and the results are publicized, schools can no longer hide from subpar scores. "It's undeniable that the push for more testing shined light on things we didn't know before,"[15] says Sandi Jacobs, vice president of the National Council on Teacher Quality, an advocacy group that presses to use student test scores as one key metric for evaluating teacher performance. Adds Sandy Kress, a lawyer and adviser to President George W. Bush, "We fly blind without objective measures."[16]

Others disagree and say the role of standardized testing in schools has grown too large. Testing critics point out that many standardized tests are not fair or objective because there is bias in the selection and presentation of questions or in the subject matter being tested. Many teachers criticize the heavy emphasis on testing, saying that it forces them to narrow their classroom

Many teachers believe that standardized testing is meant to force them to prepare students to take the tests and that the tests are culturally biased.

curriculum and teach to the test. Even some parents have pushed back, saying that too much testing has become detrimental to students. "I see frustration and bitterness among parents growing by leaps and bounds," says Leonie Haimson, a mother who runs Class Size Matters, an advocacy group in New York City that pushes for reduced testing and smaller class sizes. "What parents are saying is, 'Enough is enough.'"[17]

While many people agree on the ultimate goal of a quality education in all of America's public schools, the best way to achieve this goal remains unclear. What is clear, however, is that the debate over standardized testing is not going to be resolved anytime soon. According to a 2014 report on standardized testing by Teach Plus, a teacher advocacy organization, "No subject is more polarizing in education than testing. For some, test data is the essential ingredient of school improvement. . . . For others, testing is thought to dominate instructional time leaving little time for anything else."[18]

MEASURING STUDENTS AND SCHOOLS

In April 2012 third-grade students at Nan Gray Davis Elementary in Theodore, Alabama, grabbed their pencils and sat down to take the state's standardized reading test. Teacher Samantha Laurio gave the class advice, saying, "Do the best you can, but do not spend too much time on any one question."[19] The students had fifty-five minutes, plus an additional thirty minutes if they needed it, to finish the test. While the students worked, the elementary school's halls were quiet. In some classrooms students positioned blank folders to make sure the child next to them could not see their answer sheet.

Landon Hirtreiter, a third grader in the school's gifted program, admitted that he was nervous about the tests. He said he prepared as his teachers instructed. "Pay attention in class, and eat a good breakfast. I had French toast," he says. The reading test is graded into four categories. Students who receive a level three are considered proficient, while those who receive a level four are considered advanced. "I'm hoping I'll make a four,"[20] says Landon. His school is also hoping for good scores for him and the rest of the schools' students. The school will be rated under the federal No Child Left Behind Act based on the scores of students in third, fourth, and fifth grades.

Like at Nan Gray Davis Elementary, standardized tests are used in every public school in the United States, in almost every grade level. Although tests differ by state and by grade, they are all used as a tool to assess student performance. "State test results are the best evidence of whether kids know more. . . . We're trying to present solid evidence and ground the debate in facts rather than just assertions,"[21] says Jack Jennings, the president and chief executive officer of the Center on Education Policy. Standardized tests are also increasingly being used to compare schools statewide, identify gaps in student achievement, and hold schools accountable for student achievement.

Accurate Measure of Student Performance

Supporters of standardized tests say that they are a basic and objective measuring stick to see how a child is performing in school compared to his or her peers. Multiple-choice standardized tests are frequently graded by a machine, which eliminates human subjectivity, bias, and error. The answer is either right or wrong. No subjectivity on the part of the grader enters the scoring. "Research and experience show that standardized tests are generally good at measuring students' knowledge, skills, and understandings because they are objective, fair, efficient, and comprehensive,"[22] says Herbert J. Walberg, a distinguished visiting fellow at the Hoover Institution and former professor at Harvard and the University of Illinois–Chicago who has written extensively about measuring and raising student achievement and human accomplishments.

Standardized tests can also provide critical information about a student's specific educational needs. Using the test results, parents and teachers identify areas of strength and weakness and develop a plan to help an individual student. "School reading and mathematics skills, for example, can be precisely specified and as students learn the skills, they benefit from ongoing information tailored to their specific individual progress," says Walberg. "Computers streamline this process by providing immediate feedback about correct and incorrect responses far more quickly and with much greater patience than teachers and tutors can provide."[23]

Testing Alone Is Insufficient

At the same time, some people are convinced that standardized tests are being relied on too heavily in schools to evaluate student performance. They argue that how a student performs on a multiple-choice test is only one facet of a child's learning profile and that testing alone cannot accurately assess whether a child is learning and progressing in school. Critics point out that standardized tests evaluate a student's memorization of rote facts but do little to assess a child's creativity or problem-solving skills. For example, on a multiple-choice math test, one child may get a question wrong because he does not understand the problem. Another child may answer incorrectly because she made a simple error in a multistep problem, even though she understands the correct sequence of steps. In this case the two children will be scored identically even though their understanding of the subject vastly differs.

In addition, critics say many test questions are too simple for students to demonstrate sophisticated reading comprehension and critical thinking. For example, memorizing rote facts to pass a multiple-choice social studies test does not indicate if a student understands the historical implications and consequences of past events. In a 2013 speech to the American Educational Research

Standardized testing, proponents claim, provides critical information about a student's specific educational needs.

Association, Secretary of Education Arne Duncan acknowledged the shortcomings of standardized tests. "State assessments in mathematics and English often fail to capture the full spectrum of what students know and can do," he said. "Students, parents, and educators know there is much more to a sound education than picking the right answer on a multiple-choice question."[24]

Julia Fox is a high school student at Casa Grande High School in Petaluma, California. She agrees that testing should only be one part of assessing what students can achieve. Says Fox:

> No Child Left Behind was established just as I was going into kindergarten, so I've grown up with this law. I've always ended the school year with the required tests, so I've never known anything different. Tests are important, but are not the only way to find out what kids can do. I know I am not the best test taker, so multiple choice tests aren't always the best way to show my abilities. And I wouldn't want to just learn how to score better on them.[25]

Many private schools in the United States, most of which are exempt from the No Child Left Behind testing provisions, use a broader approach to evaluating student performance. Educators combine information from standardized testing, formative assessments that identify skills that a student needs reinforced, and an overall assessment of a student's work. Advocates say this balanced approach to evaluating students creates a more complete picture of a student's achievement over time and helps determine how well prepared they are for the future. Patrick Bassett, president of the National Association of Independent Schools, a nonprofit organization for private schools, explains:

> At the end of the day, students—in public, independent, private and charter schools—succeed where there is an intentional, serious and individualized culture that cares deeply about kids and their studies. Testing is one way to measure what happens in schools, but it should not be the focus of school. When we create student-centered and highly engaging school environments where students are excited about learning, students succeed, not just on this year's tests, but in life.[26]

US secretary of education Arne Duncan has acknowledged the shortcomings of standardized testing, saying, "State assessments in mathematics and English often fail to capture the full spectrum of what students know and can do."

Bias in Tests

Many people are concerned about the potential for cultural, language, and socioeconomic bias in standardized tests that can cause certain groups of students to score lower. For example, nonnative English speakers may be disadvantaged on a reading comprehension test if their command of the English language is not as strong as that of a native English-speaking student. Other biases can arise when standardized tests ask students to use knowledge about the world that they typically do not learn in school. For example, an essay question may ask a student to write about fishing. A child who grows up in an urban setting may never have been fishing and have no experience on which to draw to answer the question. As a result of these test biases, some groups of students, including certain minority groups and nonnative English speakers, can be at a disadvantage before they even answer the test's first question.

Pumped Up for Testing

In some schools teachers and students are using unique methods to get ready for standardized tests. At Gilliard Elementary in Alabama, students and teachers changed the lyrics of popular songs and created others to pump them up for the test. They recorded a video of students and teachers dancing to the test-inspired songs. In the video, someone sings, "It was so much work, but now it's clear you learned enough. . . . We know it wasn't fun, but it'll be worth it once we see our tears when we get those ARMT scores. . . . You tried with all your might. You know your success won't stop. Your scores put our school on top. You put our school on top." Gilliard's strategy of getting students energized for testing might be working. The school has been recognized for scoring higher on tests than state averages. Other schools around the country are also trying to get students excited for testing by holding pep rallies and awarding prizes to students who are in school for all days of the tests.

Quoted in Rena Havner Philips. "Mobile County Students Sing, Dance to Get Ready for Standardized Testing." AL.com, April 11, 2012. http://blog.al.com /live/2012/04/mobile_county_students_sing_da.html.

For a standardized test to be truly fair, a student's outside knowledge should not affect his or her score. Instead, only natural intellectual ability and what students learn in class should be factors in how well they do on the test. "If children come from advantaged families and stimulus-rich environments, then they are more apt to succeed on items in standardized achievement test items than will other children whose environments don't mesh as well with what the tests measure,"[27] says W. James Popham, an education assessment expert.

Many test writing companies have attempted to eliminate bias from test questions. However, the methods they use to detect bias may not work. In 2010 a study by researchers from the Indiana University Kelley School of Business reported that the tools used to check standardized tests for bias are flawed. Researchers created a simulation to test nearly 16 million individual samples of test scores from a sample of commonly used tests, including civil service exams and university entrance exams. These tests use student scores to predict how well a person will do in a job or college. The researchers built bias into most samples and predicted outcomes to resemble real-world results. Then they used new technology and procedures to identify bias in the scores and outcomes. Researchers discovered that the existing procedures to identify bias repeatedly missed the bias they had inserted in the data. Study leader Herman Aguinis, a professor of organizational behavior and human resources and director of the Kelley School's new Institute for Global Organizational Effectiveness, says:

> The belief in the fairness of the tests and the accuracy of the gauges to check them has been so deeply engrained that to challenge them would be akin to questioning the sun as center of the solar system.

> The irony is that for 40 years we have been trying to assess potential test bias with a biased procedure, and we now see that countless people may have been denied or given opportunities unfairly. From an ethical standpoint it may be argued that even if only one individual is affected this way, that is one too many. The problem is obviously magnified when we are dealing with hundreds of thousands, if not millions, of individuals taking standardized tests every year.[28]

Testing Stress

With so much emphasis in schools on standardized testing and getting high test scores, some children are cracking under the pressure. At test time some children have displayed signs of extreme emotional and physical stress. Educators report that children have begun crying, vomiting, or acting out from testing pressure. In 2014 Kate Wolfe, a third grader at Holiday Hill Elementary in Jacksonville, Florida, came home in tears and hyperventilating over her Florida Comprehensive Assessment Test (FCAT). Kate realized near the end of the test that she had filled out her bubble answer sheet wrong. "When I asked her about how many of the problems was she worried about she said probably about a third of the questions, which on an FCAT test is fairly significant if they end up being wrong answers whether its accidental or not,"[29] says Rebeccah Beller, Kate's mom. Kate explained why she was so upset, saying, "I thought that I was going to get a low grade because of it because those would be counted wrong."[30]

For children like Kate, testing stress can affect them physically and psychologically. Wendy Sapolsky, a Jacksonville pediatrician, says she has seen an increasing number of children with stress-related illnesses during standardized test times, usually between February and April. Patients report symptoms from stomachaches to panic attacks. "We've seen increased anxiety over the past five to eight years," says Sapolsky. "I mean, it's just incredible. Sometimes, these kids get so worked up as early as

The pressure of having to pass standardized tests has caused some students to display signs of extreme emotional and physical stress.

third grade with having to pass the FCAT's to pass third grade, that this time of year we have some children . . . that have such severe anxiety that we can't get them to school at this time of year. Literally, they will not get out of the car."[31]

IMPROVING PROGRAMS

"When standardized tests are used appropriately, a great deal can be learned about how well schools function. That information allows educators and policymakers to make better-informed conclusions about how much students are learning, which in turn allows them to make better-informed decisions about improving programs."—Herbert J. Walberg, a distinguished visiting fellow at the Hoover Institution

Herbert J. Walberg. "Stop the War Against Standardized Tests." Hoover Institution, May 20, 2011. www.hoover.org/research/stop-war-against-standardized-tests.

According to University of Hartford psychology professor Natasha Segool, too much anxiety can have a negative effect on a student's performance on tests. "If students aren't achieving to their highest potential as a result of anxiety . . . it clearly has the potential to not only affect children long-term, in terms of their achievement, but also in terms of self-concept, what they think about themselves,"[32] says Segool.

Holding Schools Accountable

Today's era of standardized testing has grown from a widespread desire to improve education in America's public schools. Nearly every state has developed standards for the skills and knowledge students should have. States have also developed tests aligned to those standards to measure student progress. Now states are also holding schools accountable for their students' test scores, to ensure states are meeting their obligation to every student. Many state programs reward or sanction schools based on the student test scores. In addition, test scores are often publicly reported, resulting in positive or negative publicity for schools.

Under NCLB each state sets its own educational goals and standards. NCLB requires every public school district to make annual progress toward the academic goals and standards set by the state, also known as Adequate Yearly Progress (AYP). The ultimate goal under NCLB was for all students in all states to meet state proficiency standards in math and language arts by 2014. Standardized tests scores are the main tool states use to determine if schools are meeting state standards.

Supporters of standardized testing and school accountability say that testing has highlighted the achievement gap between different groups of students. NCLB required schools to report test scores publicly, including information about performance of minorities, English-language learners, and special-education students. Public reporting highlighted disparities between groups of learners and pressured schools to help the most vulnerable students. "Under No Child, schools and districts were finally required to offer honest data on how well they were educating children of all socioeconomic backgrounds,"[33] says RiShawn Biddle, editor of *Dropout Nation*, an education reform magazine.

Supporters of NCLB say requiring testing increases school accountability for the performance of all students, including minorities and low-income students. If schools do not meet AYP, they may lose state or federal funding or receive other sanctions. Andrew J. Rotherham, cofounder and partner at Bellwether Education, a nonprofit organization working to improve educational outcomes for low-income students, explains:

> The law holds schools accountable for educating all students, especially those, like poor and minority students, who have traditionally been ill-served by public education. It does not require universal excellence, but it does require states and schools to close achievement gaps on state tests. That is a vital emphasis. With dropout rates of nearly 50 percent for minority youngsters and yawning gaps in achievement between white students and minority students, educational equity must be at the forefront of any effort to expand opportunity in America.[34]

Opting Out of Tests

Across the country a small but growing number of parents and students are choosing to opt out of standardized tests. From New York City to Seattle, parents and students are protesting standardized tests by not taking them. Darcie Cimarusti from Highland Park, New Jersey, did not want her twin first-grade daughters to stress over standardized tests, so she made an agreement with the girls' principal that they would move to a kindergarten classroom while their classmates took the test. Cimarusti says that she hopes her daughters never have to take a standardized test, because she sees little educational value in them. Eighth grader Tucker Richardson from Delaware Township, New Jersey, sat out tests in his school because his parents oppose the way high-stakes tests are being used to evaluate teachers and the stress it puts on students.

Others caution that parents should consider opting out carefully. Kristen Jaudon, a spokesperson for the Washington Office of Superintendent of Public Instruction, says opting out of tests can have detrimental effects on both students and schools. Parents cannot identify if children are having problems in a particular subject, while teachers and schools cannot accurately assess if teaching methods and curriculum are effective.

In many cases using tests to hold schools accountable has had a positive effect on student learning. According to data from a National Assessment of Educational Progress long-term study released in 2013, students have scored better in math and reading tests than peers forty years ago. In addition, for nine-year-olds and thirteen-year-olds, there has been an increase in test scores in math and reading since 2004, when No Child Left Behind began taking effect. The data also showed that black and Hispanic students made more significant improvement in their scores than white students, which narrowed the achievement gap. "When you break out the data over the long term and ask who is improving, the answer is . . . everyone," says Kati Haycock, president of the Education Trust, a nonprofit organization that works to close the achievement gap between poor and privileged children. "And the good news, given where they started, is that black and Latino children have racked up some of the biggest gains of all."[35]

Supporters of NCLB say required testing compels schools to be accountable for the performance of all students, including minorities and low-income students.

While most people agree that holding schools accountable is an important part of ensuring a quality education for all children, some believe that using standardized tests to rate schools is not an accurate assessment of school performance. Kevin Carey, director of the Education Policy Program at the Washington, D.C.–based New America Foundation, explains:

> School evaluation is complicated and should be based substantially on expert human judgment. In Great Britain, highly trained school inspectors consider many kinds of information, including standardized test scores, to rate schools. But they also conduct site visits, observe classrooms and interview teachers and students. Then they make a comprehensive judgment about whether a school needs to be overhauled.[36]

In some cases educators say the goals required by AYP and measured with test scores are simply unattainable. Under NCLB 100 percent of students were required to achieve proficiency in state reading and math tests by 2014. Although schools have made improvements in student test scores, many say that 100 percent compliance is simply unrealistic. No Child Left Behind "was completely out of sync with what was happening on the ground in districts," says Anne Hyslop, a policy analyst with the New America Foundation. "It was completely insane that you would have 100 percent of students in Illinois or any schools being proficient in Common Core assessments that are more rigorous and more challenging."[37]

No Improvement

"While the intentions may have been good, a decade of top-down, test-based schooling created by No Child Left Behind and Race to the Top—focused on hyper-testing students, sanctioning teachers and closing schools—has failed to improve the quality of American public education."—Randi Weingarten, president of the American Federation of Teachers

Quoted in Allie Bidwell. "Study: High Standardized Test Scores Don't Translate to Better Cognition." *U.S. News & World Report*, December 13, 2013. www.usnews.com /news/articles/2013/12/13/study-high-standardized-test-scores-dont-translate-to-better -cognition.

Recognizing that schools were struggling to meet AYP requirements, Education Secretary Arne Duncan announced in 2011 that the White House would grant waivers to relieve schools of some of the law's requirements. "The law—No Child Left Behind—as it currently stands is four years overdue for being rewritten. It is far too punitive, it is far too prescriptive, [led] to a dummying down of standards, [led] to a narrowing of the curriculum," said Duncan at a White House press conference announcing the waivers. "We can't afford to have the law of the land be one that has so many perverse incentives or disincentives to the kind of progress that we want to see."[38] To receive a waiver, states have to agree to raise standards, improve accountability systems, and implement school reforms to improve teacher effectiveness. Indiana governor Mitch Daniels applauded the waivers. "The waiver will make for a fairer system and one that focuses on what matters most: getting the whole system to perform better in terms of student learning,"[39] he said.

Teaching to the Test

Because of the pressure on teachers and schools for students to score well on state assessment tests, some teachers have felt like they have to teach to the tests. Class time is spent preparing students for reading and math tests and teaching test taking

A girl takes a math test. Under NCLB guidelines 100 percent of students were required to achieve proficiency in state math tests by 2014.

strategies. As a result, less time is available for teaching sciences, social studies, and the arts.

At Brookside Elementary School in Norwalk, Connecticut, teachers are feeling the pressure to raise test scores. Brookside was one of thousands of American public schools classified as failing during the 2010–2011 school year based on students' standardized test scores. Journalist Ron Berler, who spent a year observing the teachers and students at Brookside, says that testing affected what and how teachers taught in the classroom. He explains:

> From September until Christmas vacation, [Brookside] was like any school you would imagine. Then, once they got back from Christmas break, for the next nine weeks until testing began, it was a different animal. What they did was drop their curriculum, drop their texts, and instead study exclusively from a standardized-test prep book. Kids weren't getting a liberal arts education, but prepping to a very narrowly drawn standardized test in primarily language arts and math. Because they were interested in passing the test more than anything else, for that 22 percent of the school year, they taught primarily to the broad middle section of kids that were going to pass. Plus, the school went and reached out to those kids who they thought were on the cusp of possibly passing. So who gets left out? The kids at the bottom and the kids at the top.[40]

CHAPTER 3

EVALUATING TEACHERS

In September 2012 the teachers in Chicago's public schools went on strike for the first time in twenty-five years. One of the key issues in the dispute between the Chicago Teachers Union and the city's school district centered on teacher evaluations. In 2010 the Illinois legislature passed the Performance Evaluation Reform Act, which required school districts to make student achievement data as measured by standardized tests a significant factor in teacher evaluations. The Illinois law was crafted in response to the federal government's Race to the Top competition, a program that gave states financial incentives to make student performance a factor in school and teacher accountability systems. In reaction to the act, the Chicago school district designed a new teacher evaluation system, which was scheduled to be rolled out in the 2012–2013 school year. Under the new system, Recognizing Educators Advancing Chicago (REACH), a significant portion of the teacher's evaluation—40 percent— would be determined by student achievement as measured by standardized test scores. Teachers who did not improve student test scores could be fired.

The Chicago teachers were upset with the new evaluation system. They argued that student performance is affected by many factors outside of teachers' control. Teachers who have a high proportion of poor students, like many in the Chicago school district, may have a harder time improving student scores than teachers working in affluent school districts. In a statement on the eve of the strike, Chicago Teachers Union president Karen Lewis said there are "too many factors beyond our control which impact how well some students perform on standardized tests, such as poverty, exposure to violence, homelessness, hunger, and other social issues."[41] Lewis also warned the new evaluation system could lead to the unfair firing of as many as six thousand teachers, about 30 percent of the union's members. Lewis and the teachers union also argued that the state's rules require that only 25 to 30 percent of a teacher's evaluation score be tied to student growth, instead of the 40 percent per the REACH plan's design.

Less than two weeks later, the two sides came to an agreement and the Chicago teachers returned to the classroom. In the agreement the evaluation plan remained in the contract but was tweaked. Student scores will count for a lower percentage, no more than 30 percent, of a teacher's evaluation. Even so, many teachers are not happy about the revised evaluation system. Monique Redeaux, a teacher at Morrill Math and Science Specialty School in Chicago, says that using standardized test scores for

The 2012 Chicago teachers strike revolved around opposition to the Performance Evaluation Reform Act, which centered on teacher evaluations.

evaluating teachers still ignores the effect outside issues have on student performance. She says of her middle school students:

> They're dealing with issues like, "I'm hungry," or "I don't necessarily know where I'm going after school." There are things that happen in this neighborhood all the time. And you have to take time to discuss those things. Standardized tests don't account for any of that. . . . To hold us accountable for all of those other factors is unfair. To think that the things that are happening in the streets are not going to spill over into the classroom is very callous and unreasonable.[42]

A National Issue

Like Chicago, many schools districts around the country are revising teacher evaluation systems. For decades teacher evaluations were a subjective exercise, often completed when school administrators observed the teacher's performance in the classroom. These types of evaluations did little to recognize either excellent or subpar teachers or inform teachers about areas for improvement. Instead, this type of evaluation resulted in most teachers being rated similarly. Additionally, a teacher's effectiveness at helping students succeed was rarely considered in hiring or retention decisions.

The lack of recognition of the differences in teachers was highlighted in a 2009 study of teacher evaluations by the New Teacher Project, a national nonprofit group dedicated to ensuring that all students get excellent teachers. Researchers reviewed teacher evaluations in twelve sample school districts across the United States. They found that for most teachers, evaluations were short and infrequent, usually consisting of two or fewer classroom observations that lasted sixty minutes or less. In these evaluations less than 1 percent of teachers were rated as unsatisfactory. At the same time, 81 percent of administrators and 57 percent of teachers said there was a tenured teacher with a permanent position in their school who was guaranteed a job but was performing poorly. In addition, half of the districts in the study had not dismissed a single tenured teacher for poor

In reviewing teacher evaluations in twelve states, researchers found that the evaluations were short and infrequent.

performance in the past five years. The rest only dismissed a few per year.

At the same time, excellent teachers were also unrecognized. In districts with more than two possible teacher ratings, 94 percent of teachers received one of the top two, leaving truly exceptional teachers grouped with everyone else. Study respondents reported that 59 percent of teachers and 63 percent of administrators reported their schools were not doing enough to identify, compensate, promote, and retain the most effective

Cheating for Scores

The pressure to produce high test scores has led some teachers and schools to cheat. In March 2013 dozens of Atlanta Public School educators were indicted on multiple charges in a school testing cheating scandal. Beverly Hall, the district's former superintendent, faced charges of racketeering, falsifying statements, and theft. Other educators indicted include four high-level administrators, six principals, two assistant principals, six testing coordinators, fourteen teachers, and two others. The investigation into the cheating scandal involved at least fifty schools. Prosecutors allege that the educators were involved in a conspiracy to make student performance in the school district appear to be better than it was. They allege the educators cheated on state exams and hid evidence of cheating. The altered tests were the key measure the state of Georgia used to determine if it met the federal NCLB law. Schools with high test scores received additional federal funding to use in classrooms or as teacher bonus payments. A previous Georgia investigation in 2011 found cheating in forty-four Atlanta schools. Educators cheated on the tests by giving the answers to students or by changing answers after the tests were turned in. Many blame the accountability pressure on schools and teachers for the cheating. Trials for twelve of those indicted began in September 2014.

In 2012, former Georgia school superintendent Beverly Hall was indicted for racketeering, falsifying statements, and theft. Many other educators were also indicted.

achievement data for more than half of a teacher's rating, many link a significant portion of a teacher's evaluation to it. According to the same 2013 report, twenty-three states require that 50 percent of a teacher's evaluation be made up of student achievement data.

Most schools are using the new evaluation systems to help teachers grow and improve. The evaluations can identify areas where teachers need to focus in the classroom. Teachers have an incentive to make sure every child in the classroom is learning and none slip through the cracks. Some schools also use the ratings to make personnel decisions, helping them get rid of poorly performing and incompetent teachers. According to the Center for Public Education, teachers in thirty-two states can be fired for receiving poor evaluations. In most cases a single poor evaluation will not cause a teacher to lose his or her job. Instead, most districts only fire a teacher after he or she has been rated as low performing for multiple years and schools have unsuccessfully attempted interventions to improve the teacher's performance.

Concerns with Using Test Scores

Across the country educators and others have expressed concern about using student test scores as a significant piece of a teacher's evaluation. One of the main criticisms is that student test scores are influenced by many factors, within school and outside of school, that are not within a teacher's control. For example, research has shown that school factors such as class size, curriculum materials, instructional time, availability of specialists and tutors, and other learning resources can impact a student's achievement in school. Outside of school a child's home and community backgrounds, individual needs, ability, and health also influence achievement. Peer groups as well as prior teachers also play a role in how a child learns and scores on a standardized test.

In 2010 the Economic Policy Institute gathered a group of leading testing and education policy experts to assess recent research about the use of test scores in teacher evaluations. The group concluded that holding teachers accountable for growth in student test scores could actually be harmful instead of helpful to overall learning. When teachers face significant consequences for poor ratings, they have an incentive to focus more on tested subjects in class. As a result, students spend less time on other important areas of learning such as science, history, art, music, and physical education. In addition, teachers work less on developing children's social and cooperation skills, which will not be tested. The group noted in its report that tying test scores to teacher evaluations led to teachers being unwilling to work in schools with the greatest need or to collaborate with other teachers. The report's authors write:

> A review of the technical evidence leads us to conclude that, although standardized test scores of students are one piece of information for school leaders to use to make judgments about teacher effectiveness, such scores should only be part of an overall comprehensive evaluation. Some states are now considering plans that would give as much as 50 percent of the weight in teacher evaluation and compensation decisions to scores on existing tests of basic skills in math and reading. Based on the evidence, we consider this unwise. Any sound evaluation will necessarily involve a balancing of many factors that provide a more accurate view of what teachers in fact do in the classroom and how that contributes to student learning.[46]

Value-Added Assessment

There are many factors that affect a student's learning. Individual ability, family income level, support of parents, and the influence of peer groups can all impact a student's achievement in school. If teacher effectiveness was simply based on how a student performed, teachers of highly intelligent, motivated students with involved parents would unfairly receive higher scores than ones who teach English-as-a-second-language learners or children with learning disabilities. To eliminate these outside influences, evaluation methods called value-added measures attempt to quantify only the effect an individual teacher has on student learning during a school year.

In this lab class, the students are engaged in active study. With the advent of standardized testing, however, many teachers are now teaching to the text and offering less interactive teaching methods.

Using sophisticated statistical models, value-added measures take standardized test scores along with other student information and produce a value-added score for an individual teacher. Value-added models (VAMs) predict how well a student should perform in a given year based on individual factors. For each teacher the analysis compares the prediction at the beginning of the year to students' actual test scores at the end of the school year. If a teacher's students tend to perform better than expected, he or she will have a positive VAM score. For example, if a teacher's VAM score is 10, it means that students taught by that teacher demonstrated an average learning growth 10 points higher than expected as compared to similar students in the school or state. If students perform worse than expected, the teacher receives a negative VAM score. In many cases this score is used in a teacher's evaluation to make decisions about tenure, compensation, or employment.

DESTROYING EDUCATION

"Parents are stressed. Teachers are stressed. Kids are stressed by these tests more than parents. And when you tie teachers' evaluations to these tests, the teachers end up focusing their lessons on the tests. And that's starting to destroy elementary education."— Carol Burris, principal of South Side High School in Rockville Center, Long Island, New York

Quoted in Dean Paton. "Standardized Test Backlash: Some Seattle Teachers Just Say 'No.'" *Christian Science Monitor*, January 11, 2013. www.csmonitor.com/USA/Education/2013/0111/Standardized-test-backlash-Some-Seattle-teachers-just-say-no.

The use of value-added measures is spreading, with several states adding value-added measurement to teacher evaluations. In Washington, D.C., the district's IMPACT evaluation tool uses frequent classroom observations and VAMs to identify poorly performing teachers. The district dismissed four hundred teachers between 2009 and 2012 for poor evaluation results.

Supporters of value-added measures say it is a step in the right direction to identify and improve teaching in the public school system. Dan Goldhaber, director of the Center for Education Data and Research at the University of Washington–Bothell, explains:

There are limitations to value-added measures and, at the same time, we should not expect a perfect system.

No one wants to hear that "mistakes will be made," but we have to think about mistakes both from the teacher perspective and the student perspective. An evaluation system that is unlikely to differentiate teachers, today's system in most school districts, offers little downside risk for most teachers in the sense that they will not be unfairly judged to be poor performers. At the same time, exemplary teachers will not be identified as such (if all teachers are judged to be top performing, then the measure really hasn't identified anyone). The problem for students is that we fail to address teacher performance issues, meaning we are making the mistake of allowing ineffective teaching to go unaddressed. Value-added is an imperfect means of assessing teacher effectiveness. It has limitations, but it also clearly contains important information about teachers, and it would seem negligent not to use this information.[47]

Teacher Incentive Fund

In 2009 President Barack Obama proposed a significant increase in federal funding to the Teacher Incentive Fund (TIF), a program that supports performance-based teacher compensation systems. The funding increase, from $97 million in 2009 to $487.3 million in 2010, would greatly expand the program. Supporters of the program say the current way teachers are paid does little to attract the best and brightest to the teaching profession, especially to high-poverty schools. In many schools teachers are paid according to a fixed salary schedule that is tied to their length of service and educational degree. In order to receive a TIF grant, schools must support compensation systems that reward teachers, principals, and other educators who improve student achievement using fair and transparent evaluations based on multiple measures, including student growth. Applicants receive additional consideration if they implement a program that uses a value-added measure of a teacher's impact on student growth.

Opposition to Value-Added Measures

Teachers' groups around the country have expressed concern about using test scores in evaluations, even when using a VAM that attempts to isolate an individual teacher's impact on a student over a school year. They say that value-added measures still hold teachers responsible for influences out of their control. "Unless you completely believe that value-added takes into account at-risk students and all the things that affect student achievement, it's going to be really hard for teachers and teachers' unions to sign on to evaluation systems where the predominant thing is student performance,"[48] says Emily Workman, an associate policy analyst at the Education Commission of the States.

In a 2014 study education experts Morgan Polikoff and Andrew Porter cast more doubt on using value-added measures to evaluate teachers. The experts analyzed the relationship between VAM measures of teacher performance and the quality of teacher's instruction. They evaluated data from more than three hundred fourth- and eighth-grade math and English teachers in six school districts. The team found a weak to nonexistent link between VAM measures and teacher performance. As a result, Polikoff cautioned that VAM measures may not be useful for teacher evaluation and improving instruction. "If I had my druthers, I would say we need to slow way down the implementation of these teacher evaluation systems because we just don't know enough about the quality of these measures," he says. "And we have reason to believe a lot of the measures actually aren't very good quality."[49]

In April 2014 the American Statistical Association issued a statement that also criticized the use of VAMs for evaluating teachers. According to the statement:

> Ranking teachers by their VAM scores can have unintended consequences that reduce quality. This is not saying that teachers have little effect on students, but that variation among teachers accounts for a small part of the variation in scores. The majority of the variation in test scores is attributable to factors outside of the teacher's control such as student and family background, poverty, curriculum, and unmeasured influences.[50]

Debate over Fairness

Many supporters of education reform have applauded the changes being made to the teacher evaluation process. They say putting a system in place to reward teachers for excellent performance and identify those who are performing poorly is inherently fairer than a system that treats all teachers the same. Schools can reward the best teachers with increased compensation and promotions. "Effective teachers who are fairly compensated are vital ingredients in the reforms our schools need," says Secretary of Education Arne Duncan. "Schools need to have evaluation systems that fairly and accurately identify effective teachers."[51]

Opponents argue that it is unfair to base important decisions such as teacher compensation, promotion, and retention on student test scores. Every student brings a different level of ability and experience to the classroom. No two students have

Florida teachers and students protest Governor Rick Scott's education policies in 2011. Teachers filed a lawsuit challenging his state teacher evaluation system.

CHAPTER 4

TESTING FOR COLLEGE ADMISSIONS

On a Saturday in Belmont, California, high school students walked out of the Belmont Library, many looking stressed. They had just spent four hours completing what many believe is the most important test of their short lives, the SAT. The SAT is a standardized test used across the United States in the college admissions process. One of those students, Mara Meijer, is a Belmont high school junior who hopes to become a veterinarian. She says that she has spent many hours getting ready to take the SAT. "A lot of my teachers have said that if you don't have these scores, [colleges] won't even look at your applications," says Meijer. "I have tons of books at home that I practice over the weekend and after school, so I can work on upping my score." Even though she has worked hard to get a good score, Meijer questions if the test is the best way to assess students. "They're not exactly a fair way to show our skills," she says. "I wish they could find some way to really show what we can do."[54]

What Are College Admissions Tests?

For the majority of high school students, college admissions tests are a necessary part of applying to college. Many U.S. colleges and graduate schools require undergraduate and graduate students to submit standardized test scores as part of their applications. Standardized test scores allow admissions officers to compare students from different schools and areas of the country in a consistent, objective way.

College admissions tests date back to the late 1800s, when a group of American universities decided that they needed an objective and universal way to assess if prospective students would be able to handle college coursework. At the time, students were required to take a separate entrance exam for each university to which they applied. These universities formed the College Entrance Examination Board. Together they administered the first college admissions standardized test in 1901. Exam questions were in an essay format for specific subject areas. Students could use the scores from this test as part of their application to several different universities.

In the 1920s Carl Brigham adapted a U.S. Army intelligence test called the Army Alpha for use as a college admissions test. The new test, called the Scholastic Aptitude Test, or SAT, was administered to a few thousand college applicants in 1926. The test lasted about ninety minutes and had 315 questions that tested students' knowledge of vocabulary and basic math. By the

In 1930 the U.S. Army used an aptitude test that was the forerunner of the modern Scholastic Aptitude Test (SAT).

end of World War II, the SAT was accepted by many universities. Over the years, the test underwent several changes to become the modern SAT test. One change split the test into separate verbal and math sections, while another increased the amount of time test takers were allowed to complete the exam. In 2005 the SAT was changed again to add an essay as a third separate test section, along with existing verbal and math sections. For the new section, students are given a thesis and allotted twenty-five minutes to complete an essay that defends or rejects it. The essay is graded separately from the verbal and math tests; each section receiving a maximum of 800 points, for a total of 2,400 possible points on all three test sections.

A RELIABLE PREDICTOR OF COLLEGE SUCCESS

"Standardized tests provide a reasonably reliable barometer of the extent to which a student has been able to master the general high school curriculum in a way that will prepare her well for college."—Paul Siemens, director of Advantage Testing of Los Angeles

Paul Siemens. "SAT's Are Not I.Q. Tests." *New York Times*, December 5, 2011. www .nytimes.com/roomfordebate/2011/12/04/why-should-sats-matter/sats-are-not-iq-tests.

In 1959 Everett Franklin Lindquist, an education professor at the University of Iowa, developed the ACT (originally an acronym for American College Testing) as an alternative to the SAT. In addition to assessing math, reading, and English skills, the ACT tests students on their knowledge of scientific facts and principles. The ACT test is scored on a scale of 0 to 36. Today the SAT and ACT are the two main standardized tests college applicants take.

SAT Versus ACT

For many years the SAT was considered the gold standard of college admissions testing. Some eastern colleges preferred applicants to take the SAT. Which test a student took often depended on geography: Most students on the East and West Coasts took

The ACT, once thought to be inferior to the SAT, is now viewed by college admissions officers as of equal value in evaluating high school students' achievements.

the SAT, while students in the South and Midwest took the ACT. "Until recently, even within the admissions community, the ACT was to a degree the stepchild of the SAT," says Tom Parker, dean of admissions and financial aid at Amherst College. "So even with my own staff, I had to be scrupulous to be sure both tests were given equal weight."[55]

In recent years the ACT has closed the gap between the two tests, and college admissions offices now view the two tests on

Differences in the SAT and ACT

Although the SAT and ACT are both college admissions tests, there are differences between the two tests that may affect which one a student chooses to take. The SAT is designed to measure ability rather than knowledge. In contrast, the ACT measures what a student has learned in school, including science and more advanced math. "A third of SAT reading is vocabulary, so for students with limited vocabulary, the ACT is better," says Sasha DeWind, director at Tutor Associates in New York. "The questions are passage-based, and if you understand the passage, you'll probably get the answer right. And even though the ACT covers harder math, it's more similar to what students have done in school. The SAT is about getting the students to understand what they're being asked."

Another difference between the two tests is time. The ACT allows only 45 minutes to complete 75 English questions and 35 minutes for 40 reading questions. In comparison, the SAT allows students 70 minutes to complete 67 reading questions and 35 minutes for 49 writing questions. Students who do not work well under time pressure may perform better on the SAT.

Quoted in Tamar Lewin. "Testing, Testing More Students Are Taking Both the ACT and SAT." *New York Times*, August 2, 2013. www.nytimes.com/2013/08/04 /education/edlife/more-students-are-taking-both-the -act-and-sat.html?pagewanted=1&_r=0.

an equal basis. In 2012 more students took the ACT than the SAT for the first time, with 1,666,017 students taking the ACT and 1,664,479 taking the SAT. Analysts say this increase in ACT takers is partially due to an increase in the overall number of test takers.

The rise of the ACT is also due to more high-performing high school students choosing to take both tests. Of the twenty-six thousand applicants to Princeton in 2013, almost eight thousand applicants submitted scores from both the SAT and ACT in their application packages. At other top universities like Harvard and the University of Virginia, about 25 percent of applicants in 2013 submitted scores from both tests. Admissions officers say even more students likely took both tests but only submitted scores from one. "I don't know all the pieces of why this is happening, but I think more students are trying to make sure they've done everything they can," says Janet Rapelye, dean of admissions at Princeton. "And for us, more information is always better. If students choose one or the other, that's fine, because both tests have value. But if they submit both, that generally gives us a little more information."[56]

How Colleges Use Test Scores

SAT and ACT scores are used as one factor in a student's college application. If test scores are below the ranges of averages at the school, the student's application may quickly find its way to the rejection pile. Even so, most college admissions officers stress that test scores alone cannot get a student accepted into his or her top school. Grades and the difficulty of a student's curriculum are also important factors that help admissions officers assess how well a student will do academically in college.

Christoph Guttentag, dean of undergraduate admissions at Duke University, says Duke's admissions office uses the SAT and grades as one of three pieces in rating a student's academic credentials. "We look at the academic credentials (the scores and the grades), what's in the school profile (what courses the school offers) and what a student takes," says Guttentag. Duke's admissions office then evaluates whether a student's overall academic credentials are competitive compared to the overall pool of applicants. "Academic credentials become much less important once they're in the range of academic competitiveness," says Guttentag. He adds that SAT and ACT scores help admissions officers understand how well a student is prepared for attending college. "The SATs and other similar tests, they're useful to us in terms of understanding a student's academic preparation,"[57] he says.

Better Admissions Decisions

Supporters of the SAT and ACT claim these tests help colleges make better admissions decisions. They say the tests are fair and objective assessments of prospective students that can be used along with high school transcripts, application essays, and letters of recommendation to gather as much information as possible about a potential student. Says David Z. Hambrick, an associate professor of psychology at Michigan State University:

> The SAT works for its intended purpose—predicting success in college. This isn't to say that the SAT is perfect. You can probably think of someone who did poorly on the SAT and yet graduated summa cum laude from college. You can probably also think of someone who did spectacularly well on the SAT but who flunked out of college after a semester. Many factors not captured by the SAT—like personality, motivation and discipline—contribute to success in college. But, relatively speaking, the SAT works well.[58]

Standardized tests such as the SAT and the ACT give admissions offices an objective way to compare students from different states, schools, and backgrounds. These tests also help admissions offices reduce the impact of grade inflation at different high schools. Grade inflation occurs when one high school awards a higher grade for the same level of academic achievement than another school. Grade inflation is thought to be an issue affecting many schools in the United States. According to the U.S. Department of Education, the mean grade point average (GPA) for female high school graduates rose 0.33 points to 3.10 from 1999 to 2009. For males, the average GPA rose over the same ten-year period 0.31 points to 2.90. During the same time period, studies from ACT and the College Board, the company that administers the SAT, found that scores on the ACT and SAT did not significantly increase. This variation between GPA and standardized test scores may indicate that grade inflation is responsible for the rising GPAs.

Recent research also supports the use of standardized tests to predict how applicants will perform in college. In 2012 a study published in the journal *Psychological Science* reported that the predictive value of the SAT is strong, particularly when the test is used along with high school grades. Paul Sackett, a psychological scientist at the University of Minnesota, and his colleagues reviewed data from more than 143,000 students at 110 colleges and universities, along with data from previous research at University of California campuses and a data set of information from 41 additional institutions. The data included student SAT scores, socioeconomic status, and academic performance in the first year of college. Researchers found throughout all the data that SAT scores combined with high school grades were predictive of first-year college performance for students of all socioeconomic backgrounds. In addition, the researchers found that taking parents' education and family income into account had little effect on the predictive value of SAT scores and college performance. The researchers say the findings suggest the SAT is a useful indicator for colleges to use in admissions decisions. "The finding that SAT scores provide incremental validity in predicting freshman grades, beyond the predictive validity contributed by high school grades, and that this is true even when controlling for [socioeconomic status] supports the usefulness of the SAT for predicting first-year academic performance,"[59] write the study's authors.

Standardized tests like the SAT and ACT give admissions officers objective ways to compare students from different states, backgrounds, and schools.

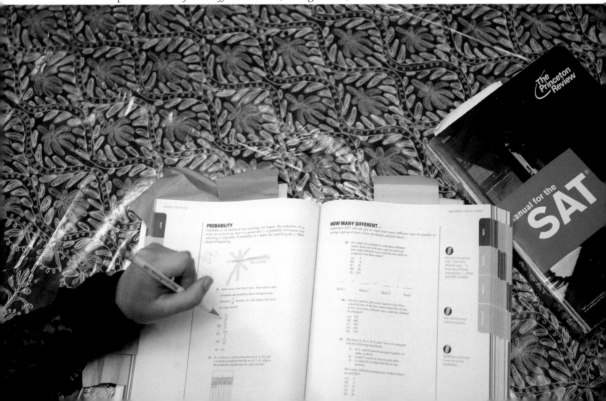

Concerns with the SAT and ACT

In recent years there has been a growing backlash against the use of standardized tests, particularly the SAT and ACT, in college admissions decisions. Critics of these tests say they have become overused and given too much weight by college admissions officers. In addition, critics claim the tests themselves may be discriminatory and biased against minorities and students of a lower socioeconomic status.

Some researchers have reported the language used in college admissions exams may be biased and favor certain groups of students. A 2010 study published by the *Harvard Educational Review* found that the SAT verbal section questions favored white students by using language with which they were more familiar as compared to nonwhite students. The study found African American students of equal academic aptitude scored lower than white students on the verbal sections. Say the study's authors:

> The confirmation of unfair test results throws into question the validity of the test and, consequently, all decisions based on its results. All admissions decisions based exclusively or predominantly on SAT performance—and therefore access to higher education institutions and subsequent job placement and professional success—appear to be biased against the African American minority group and could be exposed to legal challenge.[60]

The College Board refuted the study's findings and released a statement saying:

> The research published in *Harvard Educational Review* is deeply flawed, and it would be reckless and irresponsible to position the authors' conclusions as fact when those conclusions are based on inconsistent findings. This research utilizes only partial data sets, focuses on a student sample that is not representative of the entire population of SAT takers, and draws conclusions that do not match the data. Simply stated, this research does not withstand scrutiny.[61]

SAT Subject Tests

Every year nearly five hundred thousand students take hour-long SAT Subject Tests, according to the College Board, which administers the tests. The SAT Subject Tests are national exams that test student achievement in specific subject areas. There are twenty SAT Subject Tests in five general subject areas: English, history, languages, mathematics, and science. While many colleges do not require these tests for admission, some of the most competitive schools require or recommend students take two Subject Tests. The tests are closely aligned with high school curricula and allow students to highlight their achievement and knowledge in a particular subject area. Subject Tests also give colleges an objective assessment of a student's readiness for college coursework. Some colleges use a student's scores on the Subject Tests to help a student select the appropriate courses in college.

The SAT Subject Tests are national exams that test student achievement in specific subjects.

Others say that regardless of whether the questions themselves are biased, the way colleges use the test results is slanted against minority and lower-income students. "The problems become in how it [the test] gets used in admissions process," says Monty Neill, deputy director of FairTest. "Most colleges will use the SAT as one piece of evidence, but a lot of them will use it to weed out a whole lot of kids who never then get a chance.... So what happens is kids of color—black kids, Hispanic kids—are going to get left out. They're going to be predicted to not do well."[62]

Alternate Ways to Assess College Applicants

Critics of the SAT and ACT say these tests are poor predictors of college success. Instead of relying on a single test, colleges would be better served by using other measures such as previous grades, class rank, and student attitudes to predict who will succeed in a college setting. Alan T. Paynter is an assistant

A Bates College study found that a student's high school grade point average may be a better indicator of future college success than are SAT and ACT scores.

director of admissions at Dickenson College in Pennsylvania. He says his school uses many pieces of information to assess applicants beyond test scores and advises students to highlight their strengths over scores. Paynter explains:

> Test scores are merely one piece of a student's record that college admissions officers consider when reviewing applications. For some students, the focus and pressure placed on them to perform well on the test is so great that they miss out on highlighting the other areas we consider—the things that help build our campus communities and not just our profile. . . .
>
> This process is about highlighting your strengths and finding your right fit. So what else are you bringing to the table? Or as a colleague of mine always says, "Show us the person you are, and will be, not just the test taker you were, and don't need to be."[63]

A 2014 study from researchers at Bates College found that high school GPA may be a better indicator of college success than standardized test scores. In the three-year study, researchers looked at 123,000 students at thirty-three U.S. colleges and universities that are test optional. Test-optional schools do not require students to include standardized test scores in their application packages. The researchers compared the college GPAs and graduation rates among students who submitted standardized test scores in their applications and those who did not. They found that there was no substantial difference between the two groups. Throughout the study, the researchers found that high school performance, not standardized test scores, was the most accurate predictor of success in college. Tally Behringer, a seventeen-year-old high school senior at Deerfield Academy in Massachusetts, agrees that high school grades are a much better predictor of how a student will do in college. "There is so much emphasis on getting tutors and taking the test over and over to boost your score," says Behringer. "I feel like my GPA shows colleges what I've done over the course [of] my high school career. It shows I am dedicated and a hard worker."[64]

Making Tests Optional

Recognizing the debate over the usefulness and fairness of standardized tests, a growing number of schools have decided to eliminate the requirement for students to submit SAT or ACT scores in their applications. According to FairTest, there are currently more than eight hundred schools in the United States that do not require such scores for admission.

GRADES ARE A BETTER PREDICTOR

"A better way to evaluate applicants already exists. High school grades are better predictors of undergrad academic performance than test scores, research shows. . . . U.S. colleges and universities do not need the SAT (or ACT)—old or new—for high-quality, selective admissions."—Robert Schaeffer, public education director of FairTest

Robert Schaeffer. "New SAT Fails the Test: Opposing View." *USA Today*, March 13, 2014. www.usatoday.com/story/opinion/2014/03/13/sat-act-college-board-fairtest-editorials-debates/6387025.

In 2012 Ithaca College in New York made the decision to implement a test-optional policy for undergraduate admissions. College president Thomas Rochon says the school's internal studies showed that test scores added little to the ability to predict the success of students. In addition, Rochon says the school based its decision on the belief that requiring test scores limited their applicant pool because some potential students may choose not to apply if they are uncomfortable taking standardized tests. Says Rochon:

> As a result, we strongly suspected that we were not seeing applications from some potential students who would shine in our academic environment and who could use the Ithaca College experience as a springboard to a happy and successful life. We expected that eliminating standardized tests as a required element of the application would enable us to increase the number of highly qualified applicants to the college, increase the quality of the enrolled freshman class, and increase the diversity of that class.[65]

Rochon says the policy was a success in its first year. Ithaca's 2013 freshman class, the first admitted under the test-optional policy, was the most diverse in the school's history. He also says the quality of the students, as measured by their GPAs and optional test scores, is identical to the previous freshman class. Rochon explains:

> Standardized tests are tools rather than ends in themselves. They are often helpful as one piece of information in an application to determine whether an applicant is likely to do well in one's college environment.

> There is substantial evidence, though, that test scores for some applicants conceal more than they reveal. And when the requirement of submitting test scores deters some potentially strong students from even applying, then it is time to take a fresh look at the tool.[66]

Time and Money for Test Prep

Because of the weight placed on test scores, students are spending significant amounts of time and money preparing for the SAT and ACT exams. Many students begin preparing in their sophomore year of high school so they can take tests in the fall or spring of their junior year. Many tenth graders take the Preliminary SAT and the PLAN (the ACT's preliminary test) to see which one they do better on. Then they begin preparing. Students can buy guides to study on their own, enroll in specialized test prep classes, or hire a private tutor. They study vocabulary lists, practice problem sets, and learn test taking strategies. Students also practice by taking mock tests, attempting to simulate the actual testing conditions as closely as possible. When it comes time to take the test, some students take the actual test over and over until they are satisfied with their scores.

Sarah Rodeo, a 2013 graduate from the Hewitt School in New York City, extensively prepared for her tests but admits she struggled to juggle test prep with school and her extracurricular activities. Even though she cut back on sleep to fit it all in, Rodeo admits that she did not have the time to take a practice test each weekend like many of her classmates did. Despite her preparation, Rodeo was not happy with her SAT math scores. "I had kind of a panic attack in spring of junior year," she says. "I honest to God went into therapy to work on my anxiety about the math, because for the amount I worked, my score should have been higher." After a year of SAT prep, Rodeo decided to try the ACT. She also retook the SAT, this time scoring 90 points higher, for a score of 2150 out of 2400. "That still wasn't good enough to get me into Brown, which was what I wanted," she says. Her scores improved slightly on a third test. In hindsight Rodeo is not sure the time spent on test prep was worth it. "I'm still not sure how I feel about using all that time prepping instead of playing the piano, playing with my little brother and sister, or seeing my friends,"[67] she says.

Test prep is also costing students a significant amount of money. Test prep companies such as Kaplan and Princeton Review can charge more than $1,000 per course. Private tutors can charge upward of $15,000 a year. These prices can push test prep out of reach for many nonaffluent students. To address the issue, the College Board announced a partnership in 2014 with the nonprofit, online-based Khan Academy to provide all students with free test prep materials. The Khan Academy has provided free test prep videos for the SAT and other tests since 2006. It will now work directly with the College Board on test exercises and instructional videos in order to combat unequal access to test prep resources for lower-income students. While many applaud the changes, some experts are skeptical that it will make a real difference. "This initiative is not likely to make a dent in inequality," says Robert Schaeffer, public education director for FairTest. He says now that "everybody will have a basic level of test prep," wealthy parents will "seek out the best, most personalized test prep money can buy." Schaeffer adds, "There will always be a demand for higher quality, personalized service. Individualized lessons are better than group lessons. And they're a heck of a lot better than online videos."[68]

College admissions tests like the SAT and ACT have been a rite of passage for high school students for decades. Many say

A lucrative business has sprung up around preparing students to take the SAT.

these tests are a valuable tool for colleges to evaluate thousands of applicants from schools nationwide. Yet rising concerns over the fairness and usefulness of these tests has led to a growing call for the tests to be eliminated in favor of other evaluation tools such as grades, recommendations, and other information in a student's portfolio. "Human intelligence is so multifaceted, so complex, so varied, that no standardized testing system can be expected to capture it,"[69] says William Hiss, the former dean of admissions at Bates College in Lewiston, Maine, one of the nation's first test-optional schools.

CHAPTER 5

THE FUTURE OF STANDARDIZED TESTING

Despite an increased focus on student achievement, the effectiveness of public school systems is still an issue in the United States. Although most people agree that schools need to help students achieve their potential, how to accomplish this and how to measure it are under debate. Supporters admit standardized tests are not a perfect measure of student performance, but many people believe these tests have some value and will continue in the future. Yet as protests mount over testing, the future form, frequency, and purpose of standardized tests remains uncertain.

Future of No Child Left Behind

The 2002 No Child Left Behind Act ushered in an era of increased standardized testing throughout the United States. Although NCLB expired in 2007, its provisions remain in place until a replacement is passed. More than ten years after it was enacted, many people agree NCLB needs to be overhauled. In 2012 the House of Representatives passed legislation in an attempt to replace NCLB. The proposed Student Success Act reduced federal involvement in education issues. The House bill also eliminated the testing and teacher evaluation systems required under NCLB. Instead, states and school districts would be responsible for developing their own accountability systems. Actions and improvement plans for poorly performing schools would be handled by the states, instead of the federal government. "This legislation will restore local control, empower parents, eliminate unnecessary Washington red tape and intrusion in schools and support innovation and excellence in the classroom,"[70] says John Kline, House Education and the Workforce Committee chair and representative from Minnesota.

Critics of the House bill asserted that by removing federal accountability provisions, the bill would put the needs of minority students, low-income students, English language learners, and students with disabilities at risk of being ignored by schools. "This bill guts funding for public education, abdicates the federal government's responsibility to ensure every child has an equal opportunity to a quality education, and it walks away from our duty to hold school systems accountable,"[71] says Representative George Miller of California, who voted against the bill. As of late 2014, gridlock in Congress had stalled the House bill, along with the Senate attempts to create and pass new legislation to replace NCLB.

US Speaker of the House of Representatives John Boehner meets the press after the House passed the Student Success Act in 2013 to replace the No Child Left Behind Act.

Changing Standards

In the coming years students will be measured against changing standards. In 2010 the National Governors Association and the Council of Chief State School Officers, along with education experts across the United States, created a new set of school standards called the Common Core State Standards. The Common Core Standards are a set of math and English language arts standards that define what skills students are expected to master from kindergarten through twelfth grade. The Common Core

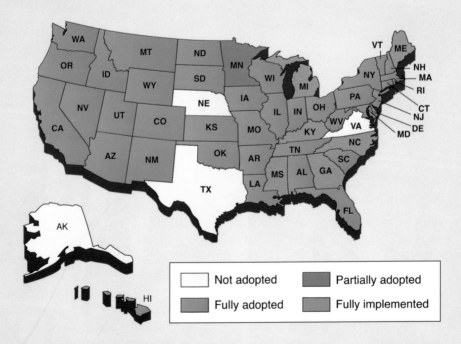

Common Core State Standards

A look at what each state has done with the national curriculum standards.

Legend:
- Not adopted
- Fully adopted
- Partially adopted
- Fully implemented

Taken from: Common Core Standards Initiative. Megan Banta, TheStatehouseFile.com.

State Standards Initiative website explains some of the benefits of the standards:

> High standards that are consistent across states provide teachers, parents, and students with a set of clear expectations to ensure that all students have the skills and knowledge necessary to succeed in college, career, and life upon graduation from high school, regardless of where they live. These standards are aligned to the expectations of colleges, workforce training programs, and employers. The standards promote equity by ensuring all students are well prepared to collaborate and compete with their peers in the United States and abroad. Unlike previous state standards, which varied widely from state to state, the Common Core enables collaboration among states on a range of tools and policies.[72]

The Common Core standards set a benchmark for math and English achievement for each grade level. Since 2010 forty-three states and Washington, D.C., have adopted the Common Core standards.

Many education leaders support the new standards, saying they will be able to replace a multitude of state standards with one set of rigorous goals for all students. In a statement about the Common Core standards, Randi Weingarten, president of the American Federation of Teachers, explains:

> These standards should affect teaching and learning in classrooms across the country. They are essential building blocks for a better education system—not a new educational fad—and they can help prepare all children, regardless of where they live, for success in college, careers and life. . . .

> Establishing these standards is a critical first step, and now the real work begins. We need to use these standards as the foundation for better schools, but we must do more—as the countries we compete with do. With common standards as the foundation, these countries provide

The Next Generation Science Standards present challenges for assessment, but they are also an opportunity to address longstanding limitations with current approaches. Current assessments tend to ask students to define the scientific method absent specific content; assessments under NGSS should ask students to demonstrate that they understand aspects of scientific reasoning by applying particular science practices, such as designing a study or interpreting the meaning of a data set, to questions about genetic inheritance, for example.[77]

In 2013 the National Research Council released a report that recommended a new system of assessments be developed after NGSS adoption. It also recommended that states use information

Fourth graders participate in a fingerprint investigation to help introduce them to the scientific method as part of the Next Generation Science Standards.

from other state standardized tests and classroom assessments to measure student learning. Committee cochair Mark Wilson, professor of policy, organization, measurement, and evaluation and of cognition and development in the Graduate School of Education at the University of California–Berkeley, explains:

> It will take time to implement the new system of assessments, just as it will take time to implement the teaching approaches needed for students to learn science in the way NGSS envisions. States should develop and implement the new assessments gradually, starting with what is necessary and possible in the short term while establishing long-term goals for reaching a fully integrated system of curriculum, instruction, and assessment.[78]

Changing Tests

As state standards change, the standardized tests and assessment systems used to measure student learning are also changing. Beginning in the 2014–2015 school year, nearly every state was required to have new assessments ready to reflect the Common Core State Standards or other college and career-ready assessments they have adopted. Many states have chosen to participate in one of two state-led consortia, the Partnership for Assessment of Readiness for College and Careers (PARCC) and the Smarter Balanced Assessment Consortium, to develop new tests. These federally funded organizations are working to develop meaningful assessments that are aligned with Common Core standards. As of June 2014 nine states plus the District of Columbia planned to use PARCC assessments, seventeen planned to use Smarter Balanced exams, and eighteen states planned to use other tests. Another six states, including New York and Massachusetts, remained undecided about which tests they will use.

The organizations say they are developing more-thoughtful exams designed to promote critical thinking and problem solving, which are also goals of the Common Core standards. The new tests are computer based, which allows designers to incorporate more types of questions. Some multiple-choice questions will remain, but there will also be more complicated testing questions that allow students to demonstrate mastery of more-challenging concepts. For example, one question from a Smarter Balanced assessment asks students to read a passage and select three sentences that demonstrate that the narrator is worried. "It's about changing the way we do testing in this country," says PARCC in a press release. "PARCC states are creating tests worth taking, made up of texts worth reading and problems worth solving."[79]

In the spring of 2014, millions of randomly chosen students in fourteen states participated in a trial run of the PARCC exam. While some schools districts felt confident that they would be able to handle the new online exams, others were not so sure. In Massachusetts some schools had few problems with the trial testing. "Technology wise, it went great," says Concord-Carlisle High School vice principal Brian Miller. "We had no issues."[80] Other schools in the state reported that the tests stretched their technical resources. Schools in Cambridge and Braintree sent letters to the state that expressed their concerns about the PARCC exams. "While we applaud the efforts of the PARCC consortium . . . the current product is fraught with difficulties that prevent it from fairly assessing students' skills and school systems' work," wrote Braintree superintendent Maureen Murray and School Committee chair David Ringius. "As it stands, we fear that it is just not feasible for us to implement this test in our district."[81]

Schools will be held responsible for test results even as teachers are still figuring out how to teach to the new standards. Since the new tests are expected to be tougher than previous tests, many educators fear that states will experience large declines in student proficiency rates.

Other complaints have emerged over the number and length of the new consortium tests. PARCC estimates that its tests will take the average third grader eight hours to complete and average high school student ten hours. In addition, students could spend more time on optional midyear tests that check to see whether students and teachers are on track. The number of students being tested will also expand. Typically, students begin standardized testing in third grade and take tests each year through eighth grade and one year in high school. Under PARCC's plans, tests are being developed for kindergarteners and first and sec-

Computer-Adaptive Testing

For years students took traditional, fixed-form standardized tests. These tests present students with a set number of questions that do not change during test taking. In recent years a new type of computer-adaptive testing has emerged that creates an individualized test for students based on their answers to previous test questions. Computer adaptive tests use an algorithm to pick test questions from a large bank of test items. The algorithm selects the next question based on the answer given to previous questions, which allows questions to be tailored to a student's individual level and abilities. Computer-adaptive tests are scored on the number of items correct and the difficulty of the items presented. Experts say that the biggest advantage of adaptive tests is the ability to evaluate all students at their own level. Students also report that adaptive tests are more interesting to take. As many states move to create new computer testing in line with Common Core State Standards, at least twenty states have said that they plan to use computer-adaptive tests.

ond graders. Testing will expand to older students as well, with planned testing in ninth, tenth, and eleventh grades.

The cost of implementing the new tests is another concern. In order to administer the computer-based exams, schools will have to invest in additional computers and broadband Internet access. The tests themselves will also cost more, with some estimates saying schools will pay approximately nineteen to twenty-four dollars per student.

Many states are also concerned with the lack of control they have over the federally funded tests. When the consortia first began developing the tests, about forty states expressed interest in using them. Today several have backed out of using the tests or are still undecided. Some states that have committed to using the exams plan to give them only to third through eighth graders and use different tests for high school students. In Michigan state officials canceled the state's plans to administer the Smarter Balanced test in 2015 and instead will seek bids from other testing companies for a new exam. Michigan state senator Phil Pavlov says

Students in Massachusetts take the online PARCC test. The new standardized test may replace other tests in English and math.

that instead of a distant consortium, Michigan officials should be in charge of overseeing tests and demanding changes if there are problems with test questions or scoring. "We're really at the beginning of public scrutiny of these testing consortia," says Emmett McGroarty, a leader of the anti–Common Core movement at the American Principles Project, a conservative think tank. "This is by no means over. It will continue to snowball."[82]

Alignment Concerns

As states debate what tests to use, teachers are concerned that kids and schools could be the losers if they are forced to take tests that are not properly aligned with the new Common Core State Standards. In Michigan second-grade teacher Julie Brill says that she is expected to teach Common Core standards to her students this year but at the same time prepare them to take a non–Common Core test that measures different skills. "It's just so crazy,"[83] she says.

Assessment experts say that states that have recently decided to develop a new test or plan to use an existing test for the new standards risk giving an assessment that is not properly aligned with what students are learning. "When you've developed a test with one goal in mind, and that target is changed, you'll have a misalignment between assessment and instruction, and that's not good for anybody,"[84] says Stephen G. Sireci, director of the Center for Educational Assessment at the University of Massachusetts–Amherst. In Iowa education leaders adopted the new Common Core State Standards but chose to use an existing state test for the 2014–2015 school year. According to Brad Buck, director of K–12 education in Iowa, a study showed the old test had a "weak to limited alignment" with the Common Core. "We want a great assessment, and we have a lot of work under way to align it," says Buck. "We recognize we're in that middle ground between the assessments and the new standards, and it's not an easy place to be."[85]

Experts say that it takes many months to design a test that uses performance tasks, evidence-based essays, and sophisticated math problems that align with Common Core standards. For states that choose to buy new tests from independent testing companies or revise existing tests, assessments are likely to be similar to the traditional multiple-choice exams that received heavy criticism under NCLB. "The closer a state is to scrapping the consortia tests and doing something quickly, the more likely those tests are to be closer to that end of the continuum,"[86] says Derek Briggs, a professor of research and evaluation methodology at the University of Colorado–Boulder.

SAT Changes in 2016

In 2014 the College Board announced it will be changing the SAT to better align with schoolwork. The board said that the current version of the SAT does not focus enough on important academic skills and has become disconnected with what students are learning in high schools. The board plans to replace vocabulary challenges with words that are more commonly found in college courses, such as *empirical* and *synthesis*. Math questions will focus more narrowly on linear equations, functions, and proportional thinking. In addition, students will no longer be allowed to use a calculator on some sections of the math exam. Students will be able to take the revised exam on either paper or computer. Scoring will change from a 2,400-point maximum to a 1,600-point maximum, while the essay will become optional and have a separate score. The new SAT is scheduled to be introduced in the spring of 2016.

In March 2014, College Board president David Coleman announces updates to the SAT college entrance exams for 2016.

Teachers, students, and children rally in Oklahoma City in March 2014 to call for less standardized testing.

Testing Backlash

As the controversy swirls over new standards and new testing in schools, there has been growing push nationwide against standardized testing. Tens of thousands of activists, parents, and students have united to urge states to stop using high-stakes tests and to reduce the number of standardized tests students face. In March 2014 approximately thirty thousand educators, parents, and students rallied at the capitol building in Oklahoma City to call for a decrease in standardized tests. Doug Stafford, a principal at Emerson Middle School in Oklahoma City, is concerned with the amount of time students in his school spend on standardized tests. He says that his sixth graders spend about twenty-seven hours being tested, all of which is lost instruction time. Science teacher Tammy Delmedico says that her eighth-grade students take six standardized tests a year, which involves a significant amount of preparation time that could be spent on learning. Jeffery Corbett, president of the Oklahoma Parent Teacher Association, also opposes the amount of testing in schools. He says:

> It is time for the era of standardized tests as a dominant force in education to end. It is time to return to creative, individualized education—and to do that, we must turn our classrooms back over to our teachers. It is time to take education out of the hands of testing companies. America spends $1.7 billion annually on standardized testing. What could be done if just half of those dollars were devoted to the classroom?[87]

MEASURING NEW STANDARDS

"What we need to have are tests that measure whether students are meeting the standards. [Testing] shouldn't be the end-all and be-all. . . . [If] you teach to the standards, the test then is an accurate measurement of where we are."—Jeb Bush, Common Core advocate and former Florida governor

Quoted in Joseph P. Williams. "Who Is Fighting for Common Core?" *U.S. News & World Report*, February 27, 2014. www.usnews.com/news/special-reports/a-guide-to -common-core/articles/2014/02/27/who-is-fighting-for-common-core.

In September 2014 Pittsburgh Public Schools in Pennsylvania announced a plan to reduce the amount of time students spend in standardized testing. "We know we want to minimize the assessments in grade K–5 so we are not overburdening students,"[88] says Allison McCarthy, executive director of curriculum, instructions, and assessment. The district plans to reduce testing in grades 3, 4, and 5 by about 50 percent. There will also be testing reductions in kindergarten through grade 2 and in grades

6 through 12. School board member Carolyn Krug applauded the plan, saying that less testing will reduce student stress and give teachers more time to teach. "This has a great impact on the amount of time our children have to learn,"[89] she says.

"Many Ways of Being Smart"

The debate over standardized test shows that there is no clear right or wrong answer on how to evaluate and measure student learning and achievement. While most agree that it is important to be able to measure how well students are learning in school,

Students look up their test scores. While some support standardized testing as a fair and objective measure, others say scores tell only one part of a student's achievement.

the tests that are currently in place remain controversial. People on both sides of the issue feel strongly. While some support standardized testing as a fair and objective measure, others argue that scores tell only one part of a student's achievement. One elementary school principal wrote a letter of advice to his students as they received their test scores. It read in part:

> We are concerned that these tests do not always assess all of what it is that make each of you special and unique. The people who create these tests and score them do not know each of you—the way your teachers do, the way I hope to, and certainly not the way your families do. . . . The scores you get will tell you something, but they will not tell you everything. There are many ways of being smart.[90]

Introduction: Standardized Testing

1. Quoted in Valerie Strauss. "Seattle Teachers Boycotting Test Score a Victory." *Washington Post*, May 13, 2013. www .washingtonpost.com/blogs/answer-sheet/wp/2013/05/16 seattle-teachers-boycotting-test-score-a-victory.

2. Quoted in Dean Paton. "Standardized Test Backlash: Some Seattle Teachers Just Say 'No.'" *Christian Science Monitor*, January 11, 2013. www.csmonitor.com/USA/Education/2013 /0111/Standardized-test-backlash-Some-Seattle-teachers -just-say-no.

3. Quoted in Diane Brooks. "These Seattle Teachers Boycotted Standardized Testing—and Sparked a Nationwide Movement." *YES!*, March 14, 2014. www.yesmagazine.org/issues /education-uprising/pencils-down.

4. Quoted in Jackie Micucci. "How Garfield High Defeated the MAP Test." *Seattle*, August 2013. www.seattlemag.com/article /how-garfield-high-defeated-map-test?page=0,0.

5. Quoted in Micucci. "How Garfield High Defeated the MAP Test."

6. Quoted in Micucci. "How Garfield High Defeated the MAP Test."

7. Quoted in Eric M. Johnson. "Teacher Standoff Stokes Debate over Standardized Tests." *Chicago Tribune*, March 4, 2013. http://articles.chicagotribune.com/2013-03-04/news /sns-rt-us-usa-education-testingbre92207b-20130303_1 _standardized-tests-school-districts-academic-progress.

Chapter 1: History of Standardized Testing

8. Quoted in Sharon L. Nichols and David C. Berliner. *Collateral Damage*. Boston, MA: Harvard Education, 2007. Kindle edition.

9. Quoted in Edward Graham. "*A Nation at Risk* Turns 30: Where Did It Take Us?" *NEA Today*, April 25, 2013. http://neatoday.org/2013/04/25/a-nation-at-risk-turns-30-where-did-it-take-us.

10. Quoted in US Department of Education. "President Obama, U.S. Secretary of Education Duncan Announce National Competition to Advance School Reform," July 24, 2009. www2.ed.gov/news/pressreleases/2009/07/07242009.html.

11. Quoted in Christina Scotti. "In an Academic-Testing Frenzy, Who Really Scores the Highest?" Fox Business, June 2, 2012. www.foxbusiness.com/government/2012/05/31/in-testing-frenzy-who-scores-high.

12. Quoted in Scotti. "In an Academic-Testing Frenzy, Who Really Scores the Highest?"

13. Quoted in Scotti. "In an Academic-Testing Frenzy, Who Really Scores the Highest?"

14. Quoted in Stephanie Simon. "Parents Protest Surge in Standardized Testing." Reuters, June 12, 2012. www.reuters.com/article/2012/06/12/us-usa-education-testing-idUSBRE85B0EO20120612.

15. Quoted in Simon. "Parents Protest Surge in Standardized Testing."

16. Quoted in Simon. "Parents Protest Surge in Standardized Testing."

17. Quoted in Simon. "Parents Protest Surge in Standardized Testing."

18. Quoted in Allie Bidwell. "Report: Standardized Testing Debate Should Focus on Local School Districts." *U.S. News & World Report*, February 5, 2014. www.usnews.com/news/articles/2014/02/05/report-standardized-testing-debate-should-focus-on-local-school-districts.

Chapter 2: Measuring Students and Schools

19. Quoted in Rena Havner Philips. "More Test Security Measures Now in Place in Mobile County's Schools." AL.com, April 10, 2012. http://blog.al.com/live/2012/04/more_test_security_measures_no.htmlPress-Re.

20. Quoted in Philips. "More Test Security Measures Now in Place in Mobile County's Schools."

21. Quoted in Pauline Vu. "Study Finds Dramatic Math, Reading Gains." Pew Research Center, June 5, 2007. www.pewstates.org/projects/stateline/headlines/study-find-dramatic-math-reading-gains-85899386836

22. Herbert J. Walberg. "Stop the War Against Standardized Tests." Hoover Institution, May 20, 2011. www.hoover.org/research/stop-war-against-standardized-test.

23. Walberg. "Stop the War Against Standardized Tests."

24. Quoted in Jasmine Evans. "Problems with Standardized Testing." Education.com, November 4, 2013. www.education.com/reference/article/Ref_Test_Problems_Seven.

25. Julie Fox. "A Passion for Learning Is Hard to Quantify." *New York Times*, July 29, 2012. www.nytimes.com/roomfordebate/2012/07/29/can-school-performance-be-measured-fairly/a-passion-for-learning-is-hard-to-quantify.

26. Patrick Bassett. "Private Schools Take a Comprehensive View." *New York Times*, July 29, 2012. www.nytimes.com/roomfordebate/2012/07/29/can-school-performance-be-measured-fairly/private-schools-take-a-comprehensive-view.

27. W. James Popham. "Why Standardized Tests Don't Measure Educational Quality." ACSD, March 1999. www.ascd.org/publications/educational-leadership/Why-Standardized-Tests-Dont-Measure-Educational-Quality.aspx.

28. Quoted in Indiana University. "Tools That Assess Bias in Standardized Tests Are Flawed, Study Finds." ScienceDaily, July 31, 2010. www.sciencedaily.com/releases/2010/07/100730074308.htm.

29. Quoted in Rhema Thompson. "Too Much Test Stress? Parents, Experts Discuss High-Stakes Standardized Test Anxiety."

WJCT News, April 23, 2014. http://news.wjct.org/post/too-much-test-stress-parents-experts-discuss-high-stakes-standardized-test-anxiety.

30. Quoted in Thompson. "Too Much Test Stress? Parents, Experts Discuss High-Stakes Standardized Test Anxiety."

31. Quoted in Thompson. "Too Much Test Stress? Parents, Experts Discuss High-Stakes Standardized Test Anxiety."

32. Quoted in Thompson. "Too Much Test Stress? Parents, Experts Discuss High-Stakes Standardized Test Anxiety."

33. RiShawn Biddle. "Focus on All Schools and All Groups." *New York Times*, September 11, 2012. www.nytimes.com/roomfordebate/2012/07/29/can-school-performance-be-measured-fairly/focus-on-all-schools-and-all-groups.

34. Andrew J. Rotherham. "Accountability Must Be Focus of Any No Child Left Behind Overhaul." *U.S. New & World Report*, November 12, 2008. www.usnews.com/opinion/articles/2008/11/12/accountability-must-be-focus-of-any-no-child-left-behind-overhaul.

35. Quoted in Lyndsey Layton. "Academic Achievement Gap Is Narrowing, New National Data Show." *Washington Post*, June 27, 2013. www.washingtonpost.com/local/education/academic-achievement-gap-is-narrowing-new-national-data-show/2013/06/27/6c47b764-debd-11e2-963a-72d740e88c12_story.html.

36. Kevin Carey. "Testing Has Moved Beyond Filling Circles." *New York Times*, July 29, 2012. www.nytimes.com/roomfordebate/2012/07/29/can-school-performance-be-measured-fairly/testing-has-moved-beyond-filling-circles.

37. Quoted in Lauren Fitzpatrick. "Illinois Schools Get Waiver from No Child Left Behind Progress Mandate." *Chicago Sun Times*, April 18, 2014. www.suntimes.com/news/metro/26920452-418/illinois-schools-get-waiver-from-no-child-left-behind-progress-mandate.html#.U4dcRHb4JqY.

38. Quoted in Sally Holland. "White House Announces Waivers for No Child Left Behind Law." CNN, August 9, 2011. www.cnn.com/2011/POLITICS/08/08/no.child.waivers.

39. Quoted in CNN. "10 States Freed from Some 'No Child Left Behind' Requirements," February 10, 2012. www.cnn .com/2012/02/09/politics/states-education/index.html? _s=PM:POLITICS.

40. Quoted in Brooke Berger. "Don't Teach to the Test." *U.S. News & World Report*, April 11, 2013. www.usnews.com /opinion/articles/2013/04/11/why-excessive-standardized -testing-is-causing-american-schools-to-fail.

Chapter 3: Evaluating Teachers

41. Quoted in Liana Heitin. "Chicago Strike Puts Spotlight on Teacher-Evaluation Reform." *Education Week*, September 12, 2012. www.edweek.org/ew/articles/2012/09/12/04strike-eval .h31.html.

42. Quoted in Peter S. Goodman. "Chicago Teachers Strike a Push-Back to Education Reform." *Huffington Post*, September 15, 2012. www.huffingtonpost.com/2012/09/15/chicago -teachers-strike_n_1886142.html.

43. Daniel Weisberg, Susan Sexton, Jennifer Mulhern, and David Keeling. "The Widget Effect: Our National Failure to Acknowledge and Act on Differences in Teacher Effectiveness." New Teacher Project, June 8, 2009. http://tntp.org/assets /documents/TheWidgetEffect_execsummary_2nd_ed.pdf.

44. Quoted in New Teacher Project. "Nation's Schools Failing to Assess Teacher Effectiveness, Treating Teachers as Interchangeable Parts," June 1, 2009. http://tntp.org/news-and -press/archive/view/nations-schools-failing-to-assess-teacher -effectiveness.

45. Quoted in New Teacher Project. "Nation's Schools Failing to Assess Teacher Effectiveness, Treating Teachers as Interchangeable Parts."

46. Eva L. Baker, Paul E. Barton, Linda Darling-Hammond, Edward Haertel, Helen F. Ladd, Robert L. Linn, Diane Ravitch, Richard Rothstein, Richard J. Shavelson, and Lorrie A. Shepard. "Problems with the Use of Student Test Scores to Evaluate Teachers." Economic Policy Institute, August 29, 2010. www.epi.org/files/page/-/pdf/bp278.pdf.

47. Quoted in National Center for Analysis of Longitudinal Data in Educational Research. "CALDER Conversations: Test-Based Measures of Teacher Effectiveness," September 13, 2012. www.caldercenter.org/calder-conversation/calder-conversations-test-based-measures-teacher-effectiveness.

48. Quoted in Heitin. "Chicago Strike Puts Spotlight on Teacher-Evaluation Reform."

49. Quoted in Allie Bidwell. "Report Finds Weak Link Between Value-Added Measures and Teacher Instruction." *U.S. News & World Report,* May 13, 2014. www.usnews.com/news/articles/2014/05/13/report-finds-weak-link-between-value-added-measures-and-teacher-instruction.

50. Quoted in Bidwell. "Report Finds Weak Link Between Value-Added Measures and Teacher Instruction."

51. Quoted in New Teacher Project. "Nation's Schools Failing to Assess Teacher Effectiveness, Treating Teachers as Interchangeable Parts."

52. Quoted in Iulia Filip. "Florida Teacher-Rating System Upheld by Judge." Courthouse News Service, May 12, 2014. www.courthousenews.com/2014/05/12/67806.htm.

53. Quoted in *Wall Street Journal.* "Should Student Test Scores Be Used to Evaluate Teachers?," June 24, 2012. http://online.wsj.com/news/articles/SB10001424052702304723304577366023832205042.

Chapter 4: Testing for College Admissions

54. Quoted in Eric Westervelt. "College Applicants Sweat the SATs. Perhaps They Shouldn't." NPR, February 18, 2014. www.npr.org/2014/02/18/277059528/college-applicants-sweat-the-sats-perhaps-they-shouldn-t.

55. Quoted in Tamar Lewin. "Testing, Testing More Students Are Taking Both the ACT and SAT." *New York Times,* August 2, 2013. www.nytimes.com/2013/08/04/education/edlife/more-students-are-taking-both-the-act-and-sat.html?pagewanted=1&_r=0.

56. Quoted in Lewin. "Testing, Testing More Students Are Taking Both the ACT and SAT."

57. Quoted in Clara Ritger. "How Important Is the SAT? Top Admissions Officers Weigh In." *USA Today,* March 8, 2013. http://college.usatoday.com/2013/03/08/how-important-is -the-sat-top-admissions-officers-weigh-in.

58. David Z. Hambrick. "The SAT Is a Good Intelligence Test." *New York Times*, December 16, 2011. www.nytimes.com/room fordebate/2011/12/04/why-should-sats-matter/the-sat-is-a -good-intelligence-test.

59. Quoted in Scott Jaschik. "Renewed Debate on SAT and Wealth." *Inside Higher Ed*, September 14, 2012. www.in sidehighered.com/news/2012/09/14/new-research-finds -sat-equally-predictive-those-high-and-low-socioeconomic -status#sthash.0Qsq0kXd.dpbs.

60. Quoted in Scott Jaschik. "New Evidence of Racial Bias on SAT." *Inside Higher Ed*, June 21, 2010. www.insidehighered .com/news/2010/06/21/sat.

61. Quoted in Caralee Adams. "New Study Looks at Racial Bias in SAT." *College Bound* (blog), *Education Week*, June 21, 2010. http://blogs.edweek.org/edweek/college_bound/2010 /06/new_study_looks_at_racial_bias_in_sat.html?preview =1&r=2057200712.

62. Quoted in Jessica Prois. "Does the SAT Have a Racial Bias?" *Huffington Post,* April 25, 2011. www.huffingtonpost.com /2011/04/25/sat-system-needs-reform_n_853518.html.

63. Alan T. Paynter. "Test Scores Are One Piece in the College Application Process." *New York Times*, December 4, 2011. www.nytimes.com/roomfordebate/2011/12/04/why -should-sats-matter/test-scores-are-one-piece-in-the-college -application-process.

64. Quoted in Hilary Burns. "New Study Says High School GPA Matters More than SAT Scores." *USA Today,* February 26, 2014. http://college.usatoday.com/2014/02/26/new-study -says-high-school-gpa-matters-more-than-sat-scores.

65. Thomas Rochon. "The Case Against the SAT." *U.S. News & World Report*, September 6, 2013. www.usnews.com/opinion /articles/2013/09/06/why-the-sats-shouldnt-be-a-factor-in -college-admissions.

66. Rochon. "The Case Against the SAT."

67. Quoted in Lewin. "Testing, Testing More Students Are Taking Both the ACT and SAT."

68. Quoted in Nona Willis Aronowitz. "Does the New SAT Spell Doom for the Test Prep Industry?" NBC News, March 6, 2014. www.nbcnews.com/news/education/does-new-sat-spell -doom-test-prep-industry-n45936.

69. Quoted in Eric Westervelt. "College Applicants Sweat the SATs. Perhaps They Shouldn't."

Chapter 5: The Future of Standardized Testing

70. Quoted in Fox News. "House Passes Bill to Replace No Child Left Behind," July 19, 2013. www.foxnews.com /politics/2013/07/19/house-passes-bill-to-replace-no-child -left-behind.

71. Quoted in Fox News. "House Passes Bill to Replace No Child Left Behind."

72. Common Core State Standards Initiative. "Frequently Asked Questions." www.corestandards.org/wp-content/uploads/ FAQs.pdf.

73. Quoted in American Federation of Teachers. "Weingarten Calls Common Core Standards Essential Building Blocks for a Better Education System." Press release, June 3, 2010. www.aft.org/newspubs/press/2010/060310.cfm.

74. Quoted in Al Baker. "Common Core Curriculum Now Has Critics on the Left." *New York Times*, February 16, 2014. www.nytimes.com/2014/02/17/nyregion/new-york-early -champion-of-common-core-standards-joins-critics.html? _r=0.

75. Quoted in Antoinette Konz. "Sunday Edition: New Science Standards Require Ky. Students to Think for Themselves." WDRB.com, September 5, 2014. www.wdrb.com /story/26460169/sunday-edition-new-science-standards -require-ky-students-to-think-for-themselves.

76. Quoted in Konz. "Sunday Edition."

77. Quoted in National Research Council. "New System of Assessments Needed When Next Generation Science Standards Are Implemented, Report Says," December 17, 2013. www8.nationalacademies.org/onpinews/newsitem.aspx ?RecordID=18409.

78. Quoted in National Research Council. "New System of Assessments Needed When Next Generation Science Standards Are Implemented, Report Says."

79. Quoted in Sarah Garland. "Students Are Test-Driving New Common Core Exams. You Can Too." *Huffington Post*, April 11, 2014. www.huffingtonpost.com/2014/04/11/practice -common-core-tests_n_5135563.html.

80. Quoted in Sarah Butrymowicz. "A Troubled Trial Run for New Common Core Tests." Hechinger Report, June 12, 2014. http://hechingerreport.org/content/troubled-trial-run -new-common-core-tests_16321.

81. Quoted in Butrymowicz. "A Troubled Trial Run for New Common Core Tests."

82. Quoted in Stephanie Simon and Caitlin Emma. "New Twist in Common Core Wars." *Politico*, July 2, 2014. www.politico .com/story/2014/07/common-core-test-anxiety-108527.html.

83. Quoted in Simon and Emma. "New Twist in Common Core Wars."

84. Quoted in Catherine Gewertz. "Big Year Looms for Common-Core Testing." *Education Week*, September 3, 2014. www.edweek.org/ew/articles/2014/09/03/03assessment .h34.html?r=428742990&preview=1.

85. Quoted in Gewertz. "Big Year Looms for Common-Core Testing."

86. Quoted in Gewertz. "Big Year Looms for Common-Core Testing."

87. Quoted in Cindy Long. "National Movement to Curb High-Stakes Testing Gains Momentum." *NEA Today*, April 9, 2014. http://neatoday.org/2014/04/09/national-movement -to-curb-high-stakes-testing-gains-momentum.

88. Quoted in Eleanor Chute. "Pittsburgh Schools to Make Big Cuts in Testing." *Pittsburgh Post-Gazette,* September 9, 2014. www.post-gazette.com/news/education/2014/09/09 /Pittsburgh-schools-to-make-big-cuts-in-testing/stories /201409090234

89. Quoted in Chute. "Pittsburgh Schools to Dramatically Reduce Testing."

90. Quoted in Diane Ravitch. "What the Tests Don't Measure." *Diane Ravitch's Blog*, November 13, 2013. http://dianera vitch.net/2013/11/13/what-the-tests-dont-measu.

Chapter 1: History of Standardized Testing

1. In what ways has standardized testing changed over the years?
2. According to the author, what is high-stakes testing?
3. What is the difference between achievement and aptitude standardized tests?

Chapter 2: Measuring Students and Schools

1. According to the author, why are standardized tests considered an objective way to evaluate student achievement?
2. What different approaches can schools use to evaluate students?
3. Why is using test scores to hold schools accountable controversial?

Chapter 3: Evaluating Teachers

1. According to the author, what are value-added measures?
2. According to the author, why is it difficult to link student test scores to teacher evaluations?
3. How does having little variation in teacher ratings undermine the goal of improving the quality of teachers in public schools?

Chapter 4: Testing for College Admissions

1. How do college admissions officers use exams like the SAT and ACT to make better admissions decisions?
2. What concerns have been raised about college-admissions standardized tests?
3. According to the author, what alternative methods can colleges use to evaluate applicants?

Chapter 5: The Future of Standardized Testing

1. According to the author, what are the Common Core State Standards, and how will they affect standardized tests in the future?

2. Why are some people concerned that future tests will not be aligned with new educational standards?

3. What effect has increasing the number and frequency of standardized tests had on the public school system in America?

ORGANIZATIONS TO CONTACT

ACT

ACT National Office
500 ACT Dr.
PO Box 168
Iowa City, IA 52243-0168
Phone: (319) 337-1000
Website: www.act.org

ACT is a nonprofit organization responsible for the ACT test—the college admissions and placement test taken by more than 1.6 million high school students every year. ACT also provides more than one hundred other assessment, research, information, and program management services.

College Board

College Board National Office
45 Columbus Ave.
New York, NY 10023
Phone: (212) 713-8000
Website: www.collegeboard.org

Each year, the College Board helps more than 7 million students prepare for a successful transition to college through programs and services in college readiness and college success—including the SAT and the Advanced Placement Program.

ETS

ETS Corporate Headquarters
660 Rosedale Rd.
Princeton, NJ 08541
Phone: (609) 921-9000
Website: www.ets.org

The ETS is a nonprofit organization that works to advance quality and equity in education for people worldwide by creating assessments based on rigorous research.

National Center for Fair & Open Testing
PO Box 300204
Jamaica Plain, MA 02130
Phone: (617) 477-9792
Website: www.fairtest.org

The National Center for Fair & Open Testing (also known as FairTest) advances quality education and equal opportunity by promoting fair, open, valid, and educationally beneficial evaluations of students, teachers, and schools.

National Education Association (NEA)
1201 Sixteenth St. NW
Washington, DC 20036-3290
Phone: (202) 833-4000
Website: www.nea.org

The NEA is the nation's largest professional employee organization and is committed to advancing the cause of public education.

New Teacher Project
186 Joralemon St., Ste. 300
Brooklyn, NY 11201
Phone: (609) 921-9000
Website: http://tntp.org

The New Teacher Project is a national nonprofit organization that works with schools, districts, and states to provide excellent teachers to the students who need them most and advance policies and practices that ensure effective teaching in every classroom.

Books

Cynthia Bily. *Standardized Testing*. Farmington Hills, MI: Greenhaven, 2011. This title explores the issues surrounding standardized testing with contrasting pro-con essays by experts.

Dedria Bryfonski. *Standardized Testing*. Farmington Hills, MI: Greenhaven, 2012. This title presents a wide range of opinions on standardized testing.

Todd Farley. *Making the Grades: My Misadventures in the Standardized Testing Industry*. San Francisco, CA: Berrett-Koehler, 2009. This title is a firsthand account of the author's experiences working in the standardized testing industry.

Daniel Koretz. *Measuring Up: What Educational Testing Really Tells Us*. Boston, MA: Harvard University Press, 2009. An understandable explanation of standardized testing issues by a Harvard University professor.

Diane Ravitch. *The Death and Life of the Great American School System: How Testing and Choice Are Undermining Education*. New York: Basic Books, 2011. Former U.S. assistant secretary of education Ravitch critiques modern education reform ideas, including standardized testing.

Periodicals and Internet Sources

Kat Cohen. "The Truth About Standardized Tests: How They Affect Your College Application." *Huffington Post*, January 13, 2014. www.huffingtonpost.com/kat-cohen/the-truth-about-standardi_b_4588723.html. This article discusses college standardized tests and their role in college admissions.

New Teacher Project. "Nation's Schools Failing to Assess Teacher Effectiveness, Treating Teachers as Interchangeable Parts," June 1, 2009. http://tntp.org/news-and-press/archive/view

/nations-schools-failing-to-assess-teacher-effectiveness. This article discusses limitations of teacher evaluation systems.

Clara Ritger. "How Important Is the SAT? Top Admissions Officers Weigh In." *USA Today*, March 8, 2013. http://college .usatoday.com/2013/03/08/how-important-is-the-sat-top-ad missions-officers-weigh-in. This article discusses the college admissions process and what factors admissions officers consider.

Daniel Weisberg, Susan Sexton, Jennifer Mulhern, and David Keeling. "The Widget Effect: Our National Failure to Acknowledge and Act on Differences in Teacher Effectiveness." New Teacher Project, June 8, 2009. http://tntp.org/assets /documents/TheWidgetEffect_execsummary_2nd_ed.pdf. This report discusses teacher effectiveness and the value of teacher evaluation systems.

Websites

ACT (www.actstudent.org). This site offers students information about the ACT exam and planning for college.

Common Core State Standards Initiative (www.corestandar ds.org). This website offers articles and information about the Common Core State Standards.

Partnership for Assessment of Readiness for College and Careers (www.parcconline.org). This website has information about the development and rollout of the PARCC assessments.

INDEX

PICTURE CREDITS

ABOUT THE AUTHOR

Carla Mooney is the author of several books for young readers. She loves investigating new ideas and learning about the world in which we live. A graduate of the University of Pennsylvania, Mooney lives in Pittsburgh with her husband and three children.